Foster Care: Theory and Practice

JOHN TRISELIOTIS
CLIVE SELLICK
ROBIN SHORT

B.T. Batsford Ltd.
In association with British Agencies
for Adoption and Fostering

First published 1995
© John Triseliotis, Clive Sellick, Robin Short 1995

Typeset by J&L Composition Ltd, Filey, North Yorkshire
and printed in Great Britain by
Redwood Books, Trowbridge, Wilts

Published by

B.T. Batsford Ltd
4 Fitzhardinge Street
London W1H 0AH

A CIP catalogue record for this book is available from the British
Library

ISBN 0 7134 7285 5

Contents

Foreword and acknowledgements

This book was prompted mainly by students and practitioners who would often ask for a reader on the theory and practice of foster care. There is, of course, no shortage of books on foster care, but they are all the product of particular pieces of research and they did not set out to address the subject as a whole. For example, there are very interesting books on subjects such as long-term fostering, short-term fostering, specialist fostering or on foster care breakdown.

Our main aim here was to bring together in a single publication most aspects about the theory and practice of foster care, albeit briefly. The book starts with an introduction to the institution of foster care and then it goes on to examine briefly the different roles, tasks and relationships involved in the practice of foster care. These themes are then examined in greater detail with chapters on the training and assessment of foster carers, on the working relationships between social workers and foster carers and on the concept of support to foster carers. There are also two chapters on working and communicating with children who are about to move or have moved to foster care. The final chapter examines the theoretical and practical issues involved in re-uniting children with their families.

It may seem somewhat strange that three men, all with a social work and child care background, have set out to write a book on the theory and practice of fostering. The initial plan included a female co-author who sadly had to be replaced after withdrawing because of family circumstances. One of us who has been teaching students for the past thirty years or so would also like to make an admission. After so many years of teaching social work students, some phrases or sentences used in the book have become second nature, though they may have come from some other source. After using them for so long it would be impossible to identify their original author. Sincere apologies to anyone who may recognize a phrase of their own. Most of the techniques demonstrated in Chapter 8 have come from Ken Redgrave, who is a consultant in child care and who has shared in the writing of that chapter. The family figure (Fig. 13) has been contributed by Leslie London, Senior Social Worker and Nan Halliburton. It is possible that we may have failed to identify the origins of one or two diagrams which seem to be extensively used in child care work. For this we would like to offer our apologies.

A number of other people, including colleagues and secretaries have helped in the production of this book. We valued particularly the comments of Mary Beek, Gwen Gray, Jenny Musgrove, Julia Ridgeway, Joan Shireman and June Thoburn. In the end responsibility lies with us. We had invaluable secretarial assistance from Lindsay Redfern, Ann Walsingham, Olga Dalgarno, Yvonne Stables and Carol Rose.

Contributors

Clive Sellick lectures in social work at the University of East Anglia and is a Guardian ad Litem and Reporting Officer. He has been a social worker since 1976 in Children's and Families' Teams and managed a short-term fostering team in inner London. His book *Supporting Short Term Foster Carers*, was published by Avebury, 1992.

Robin Short is Child Resource Team Manager for Derbyshire Social Services Department. He has been involved in fostering work as either a practitioner or a manager since 1976.

John Triseliotis is Professor of Social Work at the University of Edinburgh. He has authored, co-authored or edited a number of books and articles on foster care and adoption. His most recent book, edited with Peter Marsh, was *Prevention and Reunification in Child Care* published by Batsford in 1993. He was awarded the OBE in 1989.

1 The Institution of Foster Care

INTRODUCTION

Evidence of informal fostering goes back to antiquity and possibly beyond. Formal, legally-sanctioned fostering, though, is of a more recent origin. Fostering itself could be defined as the undertaking by a family to look after someone else's child for a few days, weeks, months, even sometimes many years, for an allowance or fee. The basic idea behind fostering is to offer the experience of family life to children whose parents cannot do so, until the parents are able to have their child back. Though the whole concept surrounding fostering is its temporary nature, we know that for a number of reasons a minority of children will stay in foster care for many years, perhaps never returning to their families. As an instrument of social policy fostering is meant to be a service to families and children who, either because of a crisis in their lives or because of a child's behaviour, require a break or respite. Equally, fostering may be used for children removed from neglectful or abusive environments or removed from the community by the courts.

The main expectations currently placed on foster carers are summarized below:

(1) Provide nurturing and care, through the experience of family life and dependable relationships, to children whose families are temporarily or for the long term unable to do so.

(2) Recognize that children separated from their families can be in distress. Besides general high-quality care, the children require help to cope with the experience of separation and loss and possible feelings of rejection and guilt. Foster carers collaborate with the social services for the achievement of these ends.

1

(3) Recognize the temporary nature of foster care as 'substitute' care, while a more permanent home is developed for the child, preferably reunification with the family or a permanent foster/adoptive home.

(4) Include the family of origin in their dealings and talks with the child and encourage parental visits in order to help, among other things, sustain the child's identity and self-esteem.

(5) Help the child overcome possible emotional or behavioural difficulties.

(6) Collaborate with the social work services to help prepare the child for the return home, or, exceptionally, a move to adoption or independence.

The main expectation though is that foster carers will provide love, caring and reliable and consistent relationships to the children in order to promote their identity and self-esteem and their capacity to form fruitful relationships. Often they will also have to help the child overcome possible problems and difficulties. Foster carers are expected to care and love the child, whilst recognizing that one day he or she will go back to their own family or move to a new one. Carers are also expected to share their family life and affection in a way many people would find difficult. Not only are some of the demands and expectations placed on them contradictory, but they also involve complex and deep human feelings and emotions. As one of a number of foster carers put it to one of us, 'They ask you not to get attached. How can you avoid getting attached? It is people they are talking about.' Another couple remarked, 'We couldn't do it without getting involved.'

Foster carers are also asked to be patient, accept the child's family, and facilitate their visits, keep the child in touch with them, both physically and emotionally, and also work constructively with social workers towards the child's restoration to their family. It is not surprising that sometimes arrangements do not work out as intended. Most of the difficulties and failures of foster care arise because of the complex relationships involved, and the lack of role clarification for each of the four interested parties, i.e. foster carers, birth parents, child and social worker.

The temporary nature of fostering is one of its basic differences with adoption, the latter being permanent, legally binding and for life. Only long-term or permanent fostering approximates adoption, especially after the introduction in some countries of adoption allowances for 'special needs' children. The fundamental difference though between fostering and adoption must be maintained, particularly its temporary nature. Equally, foster care is different from residential care in that fostering is intended to offer deeper and more continuous relationships within a family environment.

In a piece of research carried out by Hill *et al.* (1989) children in foster care defined fostering as: 'Something happening to your family and you are then being looked after by another family for a short time or being moved around'.

The above concise definition suggests that the children are aware that something 'wrong' is happening to their families; that another family is asked to look after them temporarily and finally that fostering is associated in their minds with moves and instability. To understand the psychology of fostering it is necessary, therefore, to enter the children's ideas about ambiguities concerning which family they belong to. In addition, their perceptions convey the uncertainties of fostering and anxieties about the future.

THE HISTORICAL CONTEXT OF FOSTER CARE

Throughout human history there have always been instances of neglect, abuse and infanticide; of parents abandoning or selling their children, mostly because they were unable to bring them up themselves. Alongside this went what Boswell (1991) called the 'kindness of strangers' who sometimes would rescue such children and bring them up as their own. This was a spontaneous and informal response to the needs of abandoned or exposed children ('exposure' means the abandonment of children, mostly in the countryside, to die of exposure to the elements). Adoption in its more formal and legal form arose mainly as a response to the system of exposure, though later it was used to encompass a wider group of children. Different systems of caring for abandoned or separated children have evolved over time, but a common link between different countries has been the move away from informal to more formal systems of care, albeit at different speeds.

For example, a form of informal fostering was traditional among the Celtic and Nordic peoples which involved the placing of children in each others' families. Dispersing the children like this possibly guaranteed the survival of at least one of them from hostile attacks, plundering and raids. A more formal form of privately-paid fostering emerged in Germany around the 11th and 12th centuries, practiced mainly by wealthy families who would place their sons or daughters not only with relatives, but in other households as well (Boswell, 1991). The word 'alumni' now extensively used by universities when referring to their former graduates, was then reserved for referring to a foster child.

Phases in the Evolution of Foster Care

We can distinguish five phases in the evolution of foster care:

1. Early associations of foster care with the Poor Law
2. The placement of infants with wet nurses
3. Long-term fostering as a form of substitute parenting
4. Fostering as a temporary form of care
5. The professionalization of foster carers.

The Association of Foster Care with the Poor Law

The dissolution of the monasteries by Henry VIII, not only removed a safety net for the very poor, but left a vacuum in the education the monasteries provided for the children of the nobility. As a result, the Poor Law of 1536 and its institutions were created to respond to the needs of the destitute; and private or public schools were set up to fill the educational vacuum. Not only did the two systems provide for different groups, but whilst the public school system came to confer privelege and prestige, the institutions of the Poor Law conferred stigma on those who used them or were associated with them. The Poor Law's early connection with fostering was that of providing for the apprenticeship of children as a form of outdoor relief. A more formal boarding-out system did not emerge until the second half of the 19th century.

'Wet Nurses'

As far as it can be ascertained, the system of 'wet nurses', another name for what we would today call foster carers, has its origins probably in France around 1450. (For the account on the French system we are largely indebted to the work of Davenport-Hill & Fowke, 1889.) This form of formal fostering was meant for infants moved out of the huge residential nurseries and placed mainly in the countryside with wet nurses. The nurses were paid by the State and expected to keep the children at least up to the age of 12. However inadequate the practice may have been, judged by present-day standards, nevertheless it provided for a system of selection and pay. It is claimed that most of the children were absorbed within their foster families in a form of *de facto* adoption.

The wet-nurse system was similarly adopted in Britain by the Foundling Hospitals of London and Glasgow. An extensive system of boarding-out with wet nurses was introduced but, unlike the French system, the initial practice was to recall the children at the age of four or six. After a short period of instruction the children would be put out as apprentices. This policy of recall was abandoned by the Glasgow Hospital in 1818 when it was decided to encourage children to be brought up by the families with whom they were originally placed 'until they find their way in life'. The eventual demise of the system in Britain in the second part of the 19th century, was largely attributed to the scandals and abuses of what came to be known as 'baby farming' leading to the expansion of residential nurseries.

Long-term Fostering as a Form of 'Substitute' Parenting

As we have seen, apprenticeship and wet nursing were the nearest forms of formal fostering available. Fostering, as understood today, but long-term in nature, was introduced in Britain during the middle part of the last century. This was a more purposeful effort to board-out mostly long-term, 'orphaned' or 'abandoned' children and was pursued by both the Poor Law Boards and by voluntary organizations. In this form it lasted until the end of the Second World War. The system involved some form of selection, the payment of allowances and a nominal form of supervision. Evidence suggests that this form of fostering emerged in Ireland around 1832 and was quickly after that taken up in Scotland. Religious considerations were apparently the main motivation for its introduction in Ireland. The initiative is attributed to 'middle-class' Irish Protestants, who being a minority in a predominantly Catholic country, could not economically support institutions for 'pauper' children. Furthermore, paid fostering was thought to be preferable to institutions as it provided, in their view, 'a family-type rearing' (Davenport-Hill & Fowke, 1889).

The Borough of Paisley was possibly the first to introduce this form of fostering in Scotland, in 1838. Like their counterparts in England who followed them some thirty years later, the authorities viewed boarding-out as a long-term commitment. As already mentioned, the concepts of temporary foster care and reunification were not introduced into British child care policy and practice until after the Second World War. In fact, a number of European countries are still struggling with this idea. Other Scottish parishes followed Paisley during the next 20 or so years. The central idea was that the foster families would bring up the children as their own without interference from the natural family.

It was from this practice that the term 'substitute' parents emerged and was to lead in subsequent years to many conceptual ambiguities and misunderstandings about the nature of fostering. Additional explanations offered then, for the use of foster care, mark the beginning of a more concerted effort against the widespread use of institutions. By the second half of the 19th century, Poor Law inspectors were making comparisons in their reports between life in large and 'impersonal' institutions with the family-type care of the boarding-out system.

The popularity of fostering in Scotland could be attributed to three factors. First, unlike England, in Scotland there were fewer workhouses and out-of-door relief was extensive. There was also a general mistrust of workhouses because of the stigma they were seen to confer. Second, fostering was found to be cheaper than keeping children in institutions and third, fostering was seen as more humane. These factors are not very different from today's arguments, though some people would challenge whether foster care is much cheaper than residential provision. In Anderson (1871) we also possibly have the first study of foster care anywhere. He followed up 320 children placed by the Parish of St. Cuthbert's in Edinburgh and he declared the system a success adding that it is 'the nearest approach to the family circle'. This may have been an over-optimistic conclusion especially as the selection and supervision of foster carers was by all accounts inadequate.

England delayed this form of fostering until some years later because of the fear that it would undermine the concept of 'less eligibility'; in other words, that it would not be enough of a deterrent to families seeking state help. There were also real fears that the children might be ill-treated as had happened with the earlier apprenticeship schemes. The opposition to fostering was even greater when it came to boarding-out beyond the boundaries of the Poor Law authority. This, in their view, would have made selection and supervision of foster carers even more difficult. Today we would say that such a move would isolate the children from their social network and also make parental visiting very difficult. The final decision to board out children more extensively was not taken until 1869 when one of the inspectors reported on the advantages found in the Scottish system and this in spite of certain drawbacks concerning the inadequacy of selection and supervision (Parliamentary Papers, 176, 1870).

Semi-formal fostering and the colonies: Semi-formal fostering, used extensively by the Poor Law authorities and philanthropic children's organizations, shipped thousands of children to the colonies from the latter part of the 19th century to as late as 1956. This move served a double purpose: it helped to empty 'hard-pressed' institutions and also provided cheap labour to the homestead economies of the New Commonwealth.

Available accounts suggest that while some children found kindness, as is usually the case, many others were abused, cruelly treated and harshly exploited. Orphanages in the USA followed a practice similar to that of statutory and non-statutory agencies in Britain. Responding to the needs of their rural economies, orphanages placed children with foster families, who were mostly unpaid, except for about 10 per cent where some payment was involved (Jones, 1989).

Fostering as a Temporary Form of Care

As already mentioned, formal fostering until the end of the Second World War was largely long-term in nature with little or no contact between children and their birth parents. It was generally believed that birth parents had a bad, contaminating influence on their children and they should therefore be kept apart. Unlike previous reservations about boarding-out children beyond the parish boundaries, fear of contamination had resulted now in the placement of children tens and hundreds of miles away from their parents and networks (Trietline, 1980).

For example, Dr Barnardo's required foster parents to sign an undertaking not to allow personal or written communication between a foster child and his or her relatives or friends except with the written authorization of the Director. Hill, a strong supporter of boarding-out, is quoted by George (1970) as saying 'our greatest troubles have been occasioned by relatives, when by some accident, they have found out where the children are living and we are sometimes obliged to break off all communication' (p. 14). Yet not all fostering was arranged in distant places. Much of it, as reported elsewhere, took place within Poor Law Unions 'to avoid weakening in any way ties of family' (Twenty-third Poor Law report, 1869, p. 15). The practice of fostering children in remote areas was not abandoned until about the 1970s. In summary, the pre-1948 appeal was for foster parents who would act as 'substitute' parents to the child. The implication was that the child was not expected to return to its own family.

It was mainly after the Children Act 1948 that the concept of temporary foster care, and residential care for that matter, as a service to families and children and with the concept of reunification behind it, became more widespread. However, it took many years before it permeated social work policy and practice. Foster parents were now being asked to see the child as part of their family but also to encourage contact between parents and child, including visits; collaborate with social workers, and help to reunite the child with his or her family or, exceptionally, to go to adoptive parents. The Children Act 1948 went so far in support of fostering as to say that a child should be kept in a children's home only when it was not practicable or desirable for the time being to make arrangements for his fostering. A few years after the implementation of the Children Act 1948 there was a dramatic rise in the number of children boarded out. Disillusionment began to set in as research studies were beginning to highlight the high breakdown rates. After a short period of slowing down, a new momentum developed following the introduction of professional or specialist fostering in the early 1970s.

Unlike long-term fostering, the idea of temporary foster care made the role of being a foster carer more complex and ambiguous. Uncertainty and some confusion were now introduced about the role of foster carers and social workers and the expectations placed on each other. One major problem was that whilst foster carers were expected to be temporary carers, they saw their role as that of 'substitute' parents, often discouraging parental visits to the children. The Boarding-Out Regulations 1955 possibly contributed to this ambiguity by encouraging foster carers to treat foster children as their own, whilst also expecting them to work towards the children's return to their birth families. Though guidelines looked upon foster care as mainly temporary, nevertheless these did not stop many fostering arrangements from drifting into long-term. This was either because the parents had lost interest in the children, or they had not been helped to keep in touch with them.

Difficulties associated with fostering in the past included: the poor preparation and selection of foster carers; the complex relationships and ill-defined roles; social workers' frequent failure to encourage and assist natural parents to visit their children, and the unclear relationship between the social worker and the foster carers and that of the latter to the agency. Additional difficulties included confusion over different types of fostering; the difficulties social workers had, and still have, in estimating the length of each fostering arrangement; the tendency of some foster carers to exclude the biological family from the child's life, and the lack of contractual agreements between social worker and foster carers setting out expectations and obligations. Partly as a solution to these problems, and as a response to new ones, foster care evolved into its current stage of part-professionalization.

The Professionalization of Foster Carers

Until recently, foster care was seen as mainly suitable for 'healthy' and generally non-problematic children. It was the introduction of what came to be known as professional, specialist or treatment fostering in the early 1970s that started to shift the emphasis towards groups of children with special needs also. The idea of specialist fostering was initially used to divert adolescents who were in trouble with the courts away from residential institutions. Now it is being used for all kinds of children who present some challenge, including children moved out of institutions or those who have developmental or other difficulties. The main concepts behind this move are those of 'normalization', 'community care' and 'treatment'. The idea of normalization emphasises the right of people, including children, to live a normal life in the community. The drawbacks, particularly of large institutions of all

9

types, were well chronicled by a number of studies in the 1950s and 1960s.

Community care and family life, it is argued, avoid the uprooting of people from familiar places and people, segregating them in the care of 'experts' in specially constructed environments. This should only be done in exceptional cases and circumstances. If children have to be moved, then it is preferable to identify families from within the community to undertake the caring. Though foster care was being used for this purpose for many decades, what was being proposed now was the fostering of more 'difficult' children who previously found their way to institutions. The concept of 'normalization' also acknowledges the experience that some families have in 'treating' or handling some very problematic children, particularly adolescents. Such experience, it is further argued, can be enhanced through special training programmes.

The primary purpose of specialist fostering is to provide both care and 'treatment' rather than simply 'care'. The word 'treatment' is itself problematic, but conveys to social workers and foster carers the idea of a problem-solving approach when helping a child to manage and cope with emotional, behavioural or other difficulties. It conveys the belief that adolescents particularly could not only go to foster families but that they could also benefit from the experience. The children must be willing to participate, and to avoid the danger of the children being 'dumped', time-limits are introduced ranging from six months to about two years.

Specialist placements are also meant to be more purposefully planned than mainsteam fostering, and to be task-orientated with clear aims, expectations and methods of work. Setting goals, and the activities or behaviours required to achieve them, are also part of the process. Families are sought who possess special skills in the handling of problematic behaviour or who have skills in caring for children with learning difficulties or with some form of physical disability. Though traditionally foster carers came from what were described as 'the stable' working classes, the attempt now is to broaden recruitment. Advertisements now invite applicants to apply for a professional job with a professional fee as a reward. It is still a matter for speculation whether the attraction to a job increases if the goals are seen as challenging but not out of reach.

Though the apparent success of the first specialist programme in Kent has not been repeated in many other parts of the country, nevertheless the last twenty years have seen a proliferation of specialist fostering schemes in the UK. Sometimes, there can be other reasons why a programme may be favoured, even if its success is not as high as hoped for. Many schemes are also operating in Scandinavia, the USA, Canada and Holland. Most of these fall broadly within the framework outlined earlier, though differences exist in emphasis. For example, schemes in the UK place much more emphasis on the idea of contract and on the contribution of foster carers, particularly as a group in providing some of the support needed. Like the placement of 'special needs' children for adoption, finding, preparing and maintaining professional foster homes is also seen as requiring the undivided attention of a group of social workers who make it their job to see that such programmes succeed.

THE DIFFERENT TYPES OF FOSTER CARE

Compared with the past, there is more awareness now that there is not just one, but a number of different types of fostering, catering for different types of children's needs. In other words, the term 'foster care' is an umbrella term that covers a wide variety of situations in which a child is cared for in a family, not their own, which is receiving an allowance or a fee. Definitions of foster care, therefore, must take account of both need and purpose, but, as these concepts are rather elusive, the nearest we have come to a classification is based on the length of time a placement is expected to last. Estimates of this should obviously be based on the child's needs and circumstances, though as already mentioned, social workers do not often find it easy to estimate how long a placement is likely to last.

It is important to be clear, from the outset, about the type of fostering that is being arranged. Confusion over this can affect the selection of the foster carers and the aims and expectations of the placement. It is worth noting that Bebbington and Miles (1990) have found few differences, at least in characteristics, between those fostering 'hard-to-place' children, those providing short-term and non-specializing foster carers, except perhaps in personal motivation. Some families, as they point out, may be undertaking more than one type of fostering. This is possibly an indication that

11

the concept of specialist fostering is extending to all types of fostering and foster carers.

Below is a summary of different types of foster care (though overlaps are inevitable):

(1) Relief Care: Relief care offers hard-pressed parents, and sometimes children, a break or relief from continued care or from each other. Respite could be for periodic weekends, or for a week. It is used especially to accommodate children who have learning difficulties or some physical disability, or for teenagers who are often in conflict with their families.

(2) Emergency Fostering: This form of fostering has been introduced by a number of agencies mostly as a result of the closure of many children's homes. Emergency foster carers are expected to be available, whenever needed, to take in children for one night or a few days, until more permanent arrangements can be made. Such need could arise in the middle of the night when the police or social workers are informed of a wandering child with nowhere to stay, or a child in danger of abuse. Emergency foster carers are usually paid a fee or retainer for being available, and a separate fee for each child placed.

(3) Short-term Foster Care: This type of care could last from a few days to about twelve weeks. It can be used for any type of child, irrespective of age or difficulty and fits well with the offer of accommodation as set out in the Children Act 1989. Other uses could be for pre-adoption babies; when a parent has to go into hospital and there is no one else to take care of the children; for a passing crisis faced by a family, or for assessment purposes. No doubt some children may start as short-term and go on to become medium or long-term.

(4) Intermediate or Medium-length Fostering: This form of fostering covers the majority of children in foster care, including specialist/contractual fostering. It is also sometimes referred to as a 'Community Carers Scheme' when it is used exclusively for young people being prepared to return to their families or move to

independence. It is intended to last from about eight weeks to two years. Its aim is to give parents time to sort out their practical difficulties or relationship; as a means for helping children to overcome difficulties, or to protect a child. Again, a percentage of the children placed for a medium-length term will inevitably develop into long-term placements. Children in medium-term fostering usually require 'good enough' care and attention to their developmental needs and possibly the development of life skills. They do not require 'substitute' parents because they have parents.

(5) Long-term or Permanent Fostering: This form of fostering lasts from about two years upwards or until the child reaches adulthood. Once a placement develops into a long-term one, it inevitably becomes a form of 'substitute parenting' provided it does not exclude the family of origin. Other things being equal, it may be in the best interests of a child in long-term foster care, and who cannot return home, to be adopted by his foster carers. The provision of adoption allowances in such cases seems most appropriate. Alternatively, some long-term foster carers may be encouraged to apply for a residence or other such order to provide greater security to the placement. Triseliotis (1980) found that many children who ended up in long-term foster homes were eventually absorbed in their foster carers' families.

(6) Private fostering: Private fostering differs from statutory fostering in that the child's parents identify or secure the foster family and they pay the agreed allowance or fee. The natural parents and the foster carers have to give notice to the social services of an intended placement. Thi
the opportunity to investi
The obligation on the loca
the carers are not unsuitab ....ing provision and attention is drawn to Holman's (1973) study about the detrimental effects on children of unregulated private fostering.

The following diagram summarizes the different types of fostering discussed and possible routes for moving out:

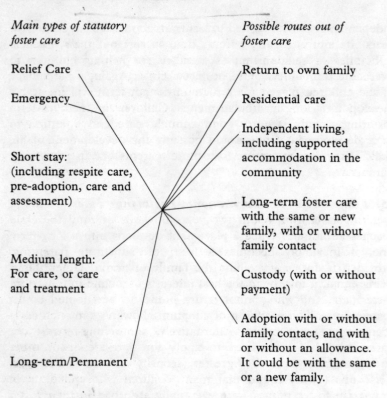

Main types of statutory foster care	Possible routes out of foster care
Relief Care	Return to own family
Emergency	Residential care
Short stay: (including respite care, pre-adoption, care and assessment)	Independent living, including supported accommodation in the community
	Long-term foster care with the same or new family, with or without family contact
Medium length: For care, or care and treatment	Custody (with or without payment)
Long-term/Permanent	Adoption with or without family contact, and with or without an allowance. It could be with the same or a new family.

OUTCOME STUDIES

All outcome studies involving human beings, and foster care is no exception, are difficult and complex to carry out, mainly because of the ethical considerations involved. As a result, it is difficult to contrast like with like, such as children of similar age, background and circumstances exposed to different forms of care. The best that can be aimed for are approximations by exploiting variations in policies and practices between agencies. Additional questions of definition and measurement can legitimately be raised about all outcome studies which purport to establish levels of satisfactory well-being, disturbance etc. Not only are these concepts elusive and difficult to define but also difficult to measure. All the methodological approaches used by different researchers such as standardized tests, self-rating questionnaires and self-reporting have their advantages and disadvantages, not to mention the possible influence on them of prevailing theories and social policies.

Who sets outcome criteria is another salient point. Should this be done, for example, by the respondents themselves, by practitioners, by those around the respondent, the researcher or a combination of these? Each and every one of these agents may have their own views about outcomes. The notion of outcomes when human beings are involved is never 'a neat package' but one with pluses and minuses. Total success or total failure can only be found with a few cases at the extremes. For the rest it is mainly a picture of 'benefits and losses' knowing that there are still many gaps in our knowledge about the answers to some important questions (Whitaker *et al*, 1985). To add to the complexities is the knowledge that between social work and foster carer inputs and outcomes there are many intervening variables which research cannot control.

Most of our understanding about the nature of fostering and what seems to work or not, has come from two types of studies. First, from retrospective or prospective studies whose main aim was to establish rates of 'success' and 'failure' and hopefully produce predictive indicators. One method that these studies have adopted to deal with the issue of 'success' and 'failure' was to take the length of time the placement has lasted as the key criterion. For example, in relation to long-term fostering, studies have taken either a three or a five-year period as the cut-off point with all placements ending earlier being described as 'failed' (Trasler, 1960; Parker 1966; George, 1970; Napier, 1972; Berridge & Cleaver, 1987).

Most studies that appeared in Britain before 1985 concentrated almost exclusively on long-term foster care (Trasler, 1960; Parker, 1966; George, 1970; Napier, 1972; Thorpe, 1973; Triseliotis, 1980; Rowe *et al.*, 1984). A common finding of these studies was that about half the children in foster care were moved on to a new placement within a period of 3–5 years with most breakdowns occurring in the first and second years. In view of these high rates of breakdown it is appropriate to ask whether the shift of resources towards foster care from the mid-1970s onward was a jusitified move or misplaced optimism. The UK Audit Commission's Survey (1981) though, found no relationship between increased rates of fostering and increasing rates of breakdowns. Whilst acknowledging that breakdowns for all forms of fostering were high, it did not find them unacceptably high.

Accurately anticipating the outcome of plans or of the length of time each placement is meant to last continues to elude practitioners. For example, Berridge and Cleaver (1987) noted that two-fifths of the children placed as short-term lasted 'significantly longer than anticipated'. A similar point was made by Millham *et al.* (1986); Wilkinson (1988) and Rowe *et al.* (1989). In the latter study only half the placements lasted as planned with 26 per cent not lasting as long and 15 per cent lasting longer (no plans for 10 per cent). Youngsters in their mid-teens were the most vulnerable for placements ending prematurely.

Irrespective of how soon or late the placement has ended, some recent studies have also asked whether the placement 'benefited' or 'helped' the child. This is not inappropriate as 'success' of the plan is not always synonymous with benefit to the child and a change of plan or even breakdown in the arrangement is not always harmful. The Strathclyde study (1988), Rowe *et al.* (1989) and Cliffe and Berridge (1991) asked this question but as answers were based solely on the views of the social worker involved, questions of validity arise. As a result, Rowe *et al.* (1989) caution that great care would be needed in presenting and interpreting some of the findings on outcomes. This is a timely caution as in their study there was significant discrepancy between the 'outcome' of the plans and the 'helpfulness' perceived to the child.

A second type of study was the 'snap-shot' approach, that is, assessing the adjustment, well-being etc. of the foster child at a particular point and time during the life of the placement (Rowe *et al.*, 1984; Colton, 1988). Only a few studies have interviewed children or adults who are or have been in foster care (Triseliotis, 1980; Rowe *et al.*, 1984; Berridge & Cleaver, 1987; Hill *et al.*, McAuley & Kelly, 1993).

SUMMARY OF FINDINGS

The following summaries concentrate on findings that are supported by two or more studies.

Short-term foster care: Approximately 40–50 per cent of children entering care experience short-term foster care. Possibly because of the short duration of the placements, this form of fostering has the highest success rate. Breakdowns among this group range from 8–12 per cent, but it is higher for adolescents (Berridge & Cleaver, 1987; Strathclyde, 1988; Millham *et al.*, 1986; Rowe *et al.*, 1989).

Intermediate foster care: Of those entering care about one-third to two-fifths experience intermediate fostering. Breakdowns among either mainstream or specialist placements average about 20 per cent in the first year and 30–40 per cent by the second and third years but significant variations exist between authorities (Berridge & Clever, 1987; Strathclyde, 1988; Rowe *et al.*, 1989). Berridge and Cleaver (1987) found a very low breakdown rate for black children placed with black families (about 10 per cent breakdown rate).

Long-term or permanent fostering: This covers the 15 per cent or so of children requiring permanency or care outside their own family. Breakdowns range from 20–60 per cent, but where it works the children seem to benefit considerably. (Triseliotis, 1980; Thoburn, 1990; Rowe *et al.*, 1984; Borland *et al.*, 1991; Strathclyde, 1991).

PREDICTIVE FACTORS

Whilst few conclusions can be drawn from the findings outlined earlier, nevertheless some patterns are beginning to form. The following is a summary of what could be cautiously described as predictive factors. It is possibly the accumulation of factors rather than the presence of a single one that matters.

1. *Child-related – negative factors*
    (a) Child very disturbed.
    (b) Long periods in residential care.
    (c) Placed in adolescence with serious behaviour problems.
    (d) Ignorance about origins, 'in care' situation, etc.
    (e) Lack of preparation.
    (f) Rivalry between fostered child and family's children (found by most studies).
    (g) Separated from siblings, though extent of disturbance in

a child is possibly a more decisive factor. (Some still tentative research suggests that children who have been sexually abused are more liable to disrupt in placement compared to others.)

(Sources: Berridge & Cleaver, 1987, Strathclyde, 1988: Rowe *et al.*, 1989; Trasler, 1960; Parker, 1966; Cautley, 1980; George, 1970; Thorpe, 1973; Aldgate, 1977, and Triseliotis, 1980.)

2. *Foster home-related – positive factors*
   (a) No children of the same sex and age or younger than the foster child in foster carers' family.
   (b) The foster carers are inclusive of the natural family.
   (c) Willingness to work with social workers.
   (d) Have been trained, prepared and are supported on an ongoing basis and have been trained to work with children who have been physically or sexually abused or are HIV positive.
   (e) Have clarity of role and expectations and they are getting enough satisfaction through carrying out their caring tasks.
   (f) The foster mother is aged 40 or over at placement. However, age of own children in family may be more important.

(Sources as under 1. above plus: Wedge & Mantle, 1991; Aldgate & Hawley, 1986; Wilkinson, 1988, and Mcauley & Kelly, 1993).

3. *Social work-related – positive factors*
   (a) Preparation and support of children.
   (b) Preparation/training and post-placement support to foster carers.
   (c) Involvement of birth family in pre- and post-placement arrangements.
   (d) Contractual approach to their work with foster carers clarifying expectations and roles.
   (e) The maintenance of children's networks.
   (f) Frequent visits to foster carers and natural parents especially in the early stages.

(Sources as under 1 above and Shaw & Hipgrave, 1983.)

NB The way the foster care services are organized does not

appear to influence outcome, but the knowledge and expertise of staff may be more decisive (Berridge & Cleaver, 1987; Rowe *et al.*, 1989, and Cliffe & Berridge, 1992).

4. *Natural parent(s) – positive factors*
   (a) Consistent visiting unless strong indications to the contrary.
   (b) Belief that they are important to their children.
   (c) No feelings of rivalry with carers or shame for their children being in foster care.
   (d) Are experiencing concrete difficulties rather than relationship ones.
   (Sources: Aldgate, 1977; Millham *et al.*, 1986; Jenkins & Norman, 1973, and Rowe *et al.*, 1984.)

Finally, and because few generalizations can be made as to who can successfully foster or who can successfully be fostered, agencies could do as well to concentrate on developing collaborative relationships with foster carers and parents, and on the preparation, training and support of foster carers. Agencies should involve parents and particularly older children in decisions about types of placement; avoid foster families with children of the same age and sex or younger than the foster child needing placement; keep, as far as possible, siblings together; recognize that placements involving very disturbed children are very vulnerable to breakdown and therefore require extra preparation and support, sometimes round the clock; encourage and support parents to visit their children, and aim to maintain the children's networks.

KEY POINTS FOR PRACTICE

- Fostering is an umbrella-type term covering different types of substitute family-care arrangements, depending on the children's needs, and the skills, wishes and preferences of the foster carers.

- Foster care has changed from being predominantly long-term or permanent, to become mainly a temporary service to families and children in need.

- The expectations placed on foster carers have also changed to include the placement of children with emotional or behavioural difficulties, physical disabilities, learning difficulties, or who are HIV positive or have AIDS.

- Though there are no firm predictive criteria of 'success' or 'failure', nevertheless outcome studies suggest certain situations which either increase the probability of breakdown or decrease it.

2 The Practice of Foster Care

This chapter provides a brief account of the major social work tasks involved in foster care work. Most of these will be expanded in subsequent chapters. The overall framework within which social workers operate is one of planning and co-ordinating work with three other parties: the foster carers, the child and the birth family. Each type of activity demands a somewhat different type of relationship, knowledge and skills. To carry out the various tasks satisfactorily, the worker has to identify with all the parties simultaneously, take in their respective points of view, their needs and how they influence and affect each other. For example, to help maintain the placement the work with the foster carers requires collaborative and consultative skills with a colleague who has the care of the child 24 hours a day. The work with the child makes demands on the worker's communication skills and knowledge about child and adolescent development and behaviour. The social work role in relation to the natural parents is in most cases to work towards the reunification of the child with the family.

The complexity of the relationships and tasks involved in foster care work, are often compounded by the ambiguities that surround them. Uncertainties, confusion, rivalries and mixed feelings carried by any one of the four parties involved could easily lead to misperceptions or confusion, or to one of the parties not being included properly in the plan or in its implementation. Having to uphold the wishes and communications of these different parties could again give rise to misunderstandings about what was said, or what the plan was or who carried particular responsibility for it. Yet the ultimate success of foster care arrangements usually depends on clear understanding about these arrangements. Studies attribute some of the difficulties encountered in foster care to ill-defined roles, a failure to define aims and clarify expectations at the start of the arrangements and to miscommunication. The increasing use by social services departments of 'link' workers to provide support to foster carers, whilst the social worker concentrates more on the child and family, could lead to new ambiguities unless close communication is maintained between the 'link' worker and social worker.

The social worker, as the agency representative, is the key and unifying figure in this dynamnic relationship, holding the situation together. He or she maintains an overview of the individuals, their situations, needs, and actions, and the ways in which they relate and interact with each other. This description appears to make the role of the social worker very powerful, yet the real skill is in maximizing the other parties' contribution and therefore their power to participate and influence events. As an example, teenagers will often say that though their views are frequently being solicited, these views are seldom considered. Full agreement about what needs to be done may not always be possible, as for example when parents and teenagers have different views, but at least there is recognition of where the differences lie.

Though the social work role may appear complex and the tasks numerous, some of the latter may have to be shared with a team of colleagues, e.g. the preparation, selection and training of foster carers, the overall planning, and perhaps the general support made available to foster carers. This can work, provided the various members of the team keep in close touch with each other, otherwise the situation could led to confusion or become antagonistic.

THE SOCIAL WORKER AND THE FOSTER CARERS

In the same way that there is no single type of fostering, there is equally no single motive for becoming a foster carer. In spite of the profiles of foster carers identified by Bebbington and Miles (1990) and referred to in Chapter 4, foster carers are not a homogenous group of people. They differ not only in their psychological characteristics but also in their background, interests and preferences. They enter their role with a variety of motives and expectations, and these eventually must be matched to the type of placement planned and the type of child proposed for placement. Foster carers have also real differences in the kinds of satisfaction they seek through fostering. They can range from the relatively private gratification of those who prefer babies to the more social satisfaction of those taking in older children. Others use the opportunity afforded them to apply existing skills to help troubled teenagers or children with physical or learning disabilities. The preferences expressed by foster carers and the skills they bring for this usually require serious attention to avoid later disappointments or frustrations. If a couple's motive is to foster a child over a lengthy period of time, eventually perhaps leading to adoption, and the agency places a child with parental contacts and high hopes of restoration to his natural family, then a number of things may happen: either the foster carers will thwart or make parental visits difficult for the child, or ask for the child to be removed, or feel cheated by the agency. Cautley (1980) reports in her study that a number of placements which have failed in the first nine months, appeared to do so because the foster carers' requests and preferences were ignored. Preferences can obviously change over time and as a result have to be kept under review. Foster carers also have different skills and as a result agencies need to have a pool of carers, to enable matching between needs and skills. Yet as Cliffe and Berridge (1991) have found from their study, the two rarely went together because of the limited number of foster carers available.

Fostering Families

Becoming a foster family demands considerable adaptations on the part of the whole family. Much of the success of the placement may rely on how well or otherwise the parents and the children have been prepared. Most families reach a kind of equilibrium in their day-to-day dealings with each other and the outside world and they are not particularly keen to see this disturbed. When a foster child is introduced, this equilibrium will inevitably be upset until each member, including the foster child, have found their place. Therefore, roles, rules and relationships will have to be renegotiated to include the newcomer.

In spite of what has been said, evidence suggests that the

children of the foster family are not always included in this vital form of preparation (London, 1992). It is worth bearing in mind that breakdown in the arrangements is more often related to the features of the placement itself and to the interactional patterns within the foster family than to the previous experiences of the foster child and his or her family. Some placements are terminated when the foster carers come to feel that their own children are suffering, e.g. through bullying or rivalry. The suggestion from London's study is that the impact of the placement on the foster carers' own children had often been underestimated. Much of the preparation was left to the parents. Even when children were thought to have been well-prepared, the arrival of the foster children came as a surprise. Apart from the host children feeling their territory had been invaded, they also found that they had to share their parents, their toys and friends. More encouragingly, this study and Von Arnim's (1988) have also found that birth children are equally willing to accept difficulties provided they understand them. The host children also found pleasure and companionship from having foster children. Very often they were the ones who helped them to integrate in the school and introduced them to new friends in the neighbourhood.

Apart from careful preparation, what also seems to reduce conflict, competition and jealousy is the maintenance of a clear distinction between the carers' own children and foster children, that is the foster children are not like the birth children but have their own families and parents and that they are mostly there for a certain period and for a specific reason. It can also be of help to foster carers to know that the care for their foster children is bound to be different in a number of ways from their love for their own children.

Clarifying Expectations and Roles

There are usually both general and specific expectations to be discussed and clarified with foster carers. As a rule, general expectations should be discussed during the training and preparatory sessions to enable would-be carers to understand the nature of the task, the policies and working methods of the agency and of the relationships involved. More specific expectations are those relating to the child being placed. Besides joint planning, the achievement of a good working relationship between social worker and foster carers will largely depend on clarity about general as well as specific aims and objectives about the placement. Foster carers also need to know which decisions have been delegated to them in respect of the child's day-to-day care and to whom they need to turn in other situations.

Expectations should not only be discussed and clarified but they should also feature in the contract to be drawn up between the social worker and the foster carers. The need for clarity of role, aims and expectations was demonstrated in the report following the Beckford inquiry (Blom-Cooper, 1986). In this case there were two sets of social workers acting somewhat independently of each other and apparently having rather different expectations from the placement. As a result different and conflicting messages were conveyed to the foster carers. Agencies and social workers who are themselves unclear, confused or uncertain about the philosophy and objectives of fostering, or about the role of foster carers and the type of fostering they are best suited for, will only convey this confusion to the foster family.

Although under the Children Act 1989 parental responsibility is shared between the agency and the parents, this still remains a rather fuzzy area. The same concept of 'parental responsibility' has given foster carers new duties requiring of them more 'sophisticated' skills and for example, extending the idea of contact to include not only birth parents but grandparents and family friends. Under the provisions of the Act, the agency is responsible and accountable for the child's welfare but it carries out its functions by delegating some of its powers to people such as foster carers. Overall control, however, remains with the local authority. In return, the foster carers are accountable to the agency for the quality of service they offer to the child. The arrangement between the agency and the foster carers has to be explicit in the agreement drawn up between them, including how accountability both on the part of the foster carers and on the part of the agency will be carried out. For example, one of the basic expectations of foster carers is to work collaboratively with the agency and its representatives. On the other hand, for foster carers to carry out their role effectively, they require status, decision-making powers and proper remuneration. While acknowledging that they are accountable to the agency, the agency, as Marsh (1988) points out, is made accountable to them for its own possible failures.

The role of the social worker in relation to foster carers has been looked at from different perspectives, something that will be discussed more extensively in a later chapter. Suffice it to say here, that with the increased professionalization and training of foster carers, the prevailing view is to regard them as members of a team undertaking some similar responsibilities as fieldworkers, but also many different ones related particularly to the care of the individual child and the relationship with the birth family. The notion of colleague or partner implies equal status and collaborative relationships, including the sharing of information, participation in all reviews, in decision-making and in planning. A truly collaborative relationship should also increase commitment.

As it is currently practised, the social worker and foster carer relationship has as its focus the child and their development and interactions within the foster family, as well as their links with the birth family. Pressures and stresses arising from the fostering task could be dealt within this relationship, though foster carers may wish to address some of these within a peer support group, something which many agencies now run. Smith (1993) adds that 'Foster parents will need continued help during the course of the placement, particularly in relation to their feelings about what is happening and practical problems which may arise, for example, with access' (p. 176).

Some Specific Expectations of Foster Carers

We recommend that these expectations are read in conjunction with the Department of Health's working party recommendations on dimensions of care and how these can be monitored through the use of charts as illustrated in the report (Parker *et al.*, 1991).

The Provision of a Parenting-type Relationship to the Child, in the Form of Nurturing and Caring

Both foster carers, in their own way, are expected to be involved in providing parenting type experiences to the child corresponding to his or her developmental needs. (This does not exclude the possibility of single foster carers if what they have to offer responds to a particular child's requirements and circumstances.) Affection, empathy and identification with the child are necessary as in natural parenthood. Because of a child's possible past separations, and other experiences, a degree of mutual attachment, which is necessary for all productive relationships, may take time to develop. As a result, foster carers require both training and support before and during the placement to tolerate the absence of quick returns. Children or adolescents presenting behaviour or emotional problems, which most do, will make more demands on the foster carers' parenting skills, patience and perseverence.

When difficult behaviours are exhibited and threaten the placement, the social worker and foster carers explore the behaviour jointly looking for possible explanations and of possible ways of dealing with it. The foster carers will have to see themselves as being involved in problem-solving, rather than blaming themselves for the behaviours. Perhaps the explanation that sometimes children react to past events or try to repeat past patterns of relating and behaving can be reassuring to foster carers. At other times, of course, some of the behaviour may be related to current patterns of interactions and attitudes within the foster family which equally require examination. A good understanding of family dynamics can enable the social worker to examine, jointly with the family and foster child, how they affect and influence one another without anyone individually being responsible. Unless there is evidence to the contrary, it has to be accepted that the foster carers share the concern about the child, and are as much interested as the social worker to understand why certain difficulties have developed. Cautley's (1980) study also highlighted how important it is for the social workers to understand how the foster mother views the child, particularly in terms of how 'difficult' some children can be. Fahlberg (1981), Jewett (1984) and Redgrave (1987) provide scenarios about such behaviours.

Because the social workers' primary concern is with the child's welfare, it is not unusual for foster carers to feel that the social worker is 'siding' with the child. Foster children, through their behaviour, may sometimes try to split not only the foster carers as a couple, but the foster carers and the social worker. Concern for the child's interests should not mean disrespect or insensitivity towards the needs of the foster family. Wires (1985) summarized the position when she says:

The worker/foster parent relationship is, first of all, a human relationship. It requires of the worker courtesy, kindliness, and an appreciation of, and a capacity for response to the foster parents' need for acceptance, recognition and status; a response to the foster parents' need to be trusted with the child; an acceptance of their desire to be good foster parents and therefore sharing with the worker in a desire for the child's welfare.

The Child's Physical Care

However uncomfortable this part of the role may be, the social worker has a responsibility to ensure that besides psychological needs, the child's physical needs are equally met. She must be satisfied that the children are properly fed and clothed, and that sleeping arrangements are satisfactory. Physical care also covers attention to health, dental and eye care and consultation on nutritional aspects. As the selection procedures are far from perfect, the social worker has to be aware of the possibility of foster children being physically or sexually abused. If this can happen to children in their own families, it should not be ruled out from this ever happening in a foster home. No doubt this notion introduces an air of suspicion into the social worker/foster carer colleague-type relationship, but it is a responsibility equally carried by the manager of any residential establishment to ensure that her staff do not exploit residents. It is for this and other reasons that it is part of good social work practice to see foster children also on their own. This is again something that should be clarified with foster carers at the outset to avoid possible ill-feeling on their part.

Educational Needs

There is a widespread view, supported also by studies such as those of Jackson (1983) and Aldgate et al. (1991) that the educational needs of children in care are often neglected and that many children leave care without any educational qualifications. The lack of qualifications usually makes it harder for them to secure suitable jobs in what is a very competitive market. A main explanation put forward for this condition is that social workers and perhaps carers expect too little of the children or that the importance of education as a compensatory attribute has been underestimated. Though attempts are now made to foster children within their immediate neighbourhoods so that they can keep links with their relatives and friends and stay on at the same school, nevertheless the realities of supply and demand often mean that children have to be placed at some distance from their home base, involving also a change of school. This places an extra demand on foster carers to liaise with the new school and the teachers.

'Inclusive Fostering' and Identity Issues

The concept of 'inclusive' fostering covers a range of things including the maintenance of links between the child and family members, knowledge of the child's origins and circumstances and an understanding of why they cannot live with their family. The fact that most fostering is temporary in nature and that it is to their families most children eventually return, highlights the importance of maintaining and promoting the links. The Children Act 1989 places considerable emphasis on the continued role of parents in the care of their children, including the need for access. The Act views continued contact as a continuum of parental responsibility. The Regulations on Family Placements also provide details on how local authorities can work, in this case in partnership with the foster carers, for the careful preparation of the child to return home and for follow-up support.

Returning to the question of background information, there is evidence that some foster children have mixed feelings about the amount of information passed on to their foster carers for fear it may be used against them or to taunt them at a time of crisis. This is more a matter for the selection and training of foster carers than an argument for restricting information. Foster carers, however, may have to be very selective in what information they pass on to their own children about the foster child. In the case of older children, social workers need to engage the young person in discussion about what is appropriate information to pass on and why. The child's views about making cetain aspects of information available, have to be respected, provided they do not put the fostering family in a difficult or at-risk situation.

The onerous demands and expectations placed on foster carers are graphically illustrated by the following comment made to Southon (1986) by a foster mother:

> To be a woman, to be a mother, to be lower middle-class or poor, to be in a minority group, to work for (with? under?) a child welfare agency, to be paid a pittance, to be asked to parent

29

a child whom no one else is able to parent, to try to love that child and to lose him when loving has been achieved, to be supervised by a 22-year-old social worker, to have to deal with school teachers, police, courts, medical appointments, angry biological parents and with the impact of all this upon one's own family – that's the lot and life of a typical foster mother (p. 50).

Somebody else could have added to this catalogue the possible allegations of physical or sexual abuse, or the foster child being HIV positive.

THE SOCIAL WORKER AND THE CHILD

The point was made earlier that the social worker is the unifying link between foster carers, birth parents and the child. Part of the task is to help in 'forming and maintaining links' between the three parties, the other part being direct work with the child. The child is the focal point. The first task in relation to the child is the creation of a structured environment to enhance the child's feelings of safety and predictability (Cipolla *et al.* 1992) and the building of a dependable relationship with the child. Second is the maintenance and promotion of a network of relationships and contacts that are of importance to the child. To achieve these objectives, there will have to be regular visits to the foster home, where the social worker will see the foster carers and the child both jointly and separately. It is surprising how often visiting social workers fail to see male carers, the children or both. Other individual relationships and contacts have to be promoted and developed as a means of rehabilitating the child, preferably with their own family or eventually with any other suitable family.

The social worker often provides a central point of support and communication for the child whose links are distributed among the birth family members, foster carers, children's home, social services, etc. If something goes wrong and the child has to be removed, as sometimes happens, the social worker is the person who can help the child to put his or her life together again. Play, drawings, life-story books, outings, activities and discussion are some of the ways for getting nearer to children. The eventual hope is that trust will be developed between the two to allow the child to share concerns, feelings, preoccupations and hopes for the future. It could be argued that, considering the frequency with which social workers move on, they are not perhaps the best people to hold these various links together. One example of poor practice was that of the foster child who, while at a holiday camp, was informed that he could not return to his foster carers because they had decided not to resume fostering. The message was conveyed by one of the camp workers. His social worker failed to turn up to explain, discuss new arrangements and begin to help rebuild the child's life. The child was left for another three days with all his bewildering feelings before he was delivered one morning to the social services offices. Another recent example which we thought was a characteristic of practice twenty or thirty years ago, was the 17 year old who only very recently found out that she had a sibling in another foster home. There is equally no shortage of examples of children in long-term foster care who do not know the names of their parents, siblings or grandparents. In contrast to these examples, was one young person who recently remarked that the social worker was the only person who stood by her during good and bad times. She added, 'I knew I could depend on him.' Another one said, 'I would have been lost without my social worker.' No doubt many other examples such as these can be found.

THE SOCIAL WORKER AND THE BIRTH PARENTS

The role and tasks of the social worker in relation to the child's parents is to assist and support them to maintain contact with the child and eventually, hopefully, take the child home. To carry out these tasks, it is necessary that the social worker maintains or develops a constructive relationship with the parents. While some parents will be glad to co-operate and work in partnership with the social worker, others may be feeling angry or apathetic. In either case, the social worker has to accept the parents' feelings or position demonstrating at the same time concern for the child and its future, something most parents usually feel too. Involving the parents in planning about their child and participating in plans and reviews (which is also required by the Children Act 1989), gives them the feeling that they are still the most important people in the child's life. Most children, even rejected and sometimes abused ones, think well of their parents. Contacts between children and birth parents have generally been found not to threaten the placement and far from it, the visits often contribute to the stability of the arrangements (Cliff & Berridge, 1991 (Borland et al.; 1991; Wedge & Mantle, 1991).

In all their dealings with the parents of children in foster care, social workers must be honest with them, letting them know where they stand and explaining, where necessary, the circumstances under which they can have their children returned. The parents should be clear about their rights, but equally about their responsibilities and obligations to the child. To facilitate clarity, and avoid possible misperceptions and misunderstandings, it is suggested that a contract be drawn up between the parents and the agency setting out the arrangements. This is also specified in the Children Act 1989, in respect of children who are accommodated. Return of the children to their families is more than an instrumental act, requiring detailed preparation, gradual re-introduction and post re-unification support.

THE CONTRACT

Repeated reference has been made so far to the desirability for a contract or agreement to be drawn up between all the parties involved in foster care, including the child (if of an age to understand). This is particularly useful for involving adolescents and teenagers. Though this is not the place to describe in depth the social work literature on the use of contracts which has been built over the last 15 or so years, the idea of contracts is being used in many areas of social work, mainly to give direction to the work done, spell out the problem to be solved, the goals to be pursued and the tasks to be undertaken by whom and how. It is meant to be open and honest and a time-limited form of social work intervention.

Further value claimed for the use of contracts is the clarity and specificity they can introduce about aims, objectives and methods, and the way they can encourage the active participation of the various parties in drawing-up the contract and the way responsibilities are allocated. Regular reviews can also provide the needed accountability from each party. Under the Children Act 1989 the agency and the parents are expected to draw up written contracts for children who are accommodated. This does not rule out the need for contracts, especially for teenagers admitted on a care order.

The contract is not a panacea for all the complexities involved in foster care work. However, for social workers, who usually find themselves in the middle of conflicting interests and ambiguous roles, the contract can be a very useful tool for the reasons outlined earlier. Our experience suggests that the probability of success is significantly enhanced when a contract has been signed between the parties involved. It is not surprising, perhaps, that specialist fostering has come to be known also as 'contractual' fostering. Something like 86 per cent of professional schemes in Britain, surveyed by Shaw & Hipgrave (1983), claim to have been using contracts. However, good intentions about contracts and actual practice may vary. Others have also noted that even adolescents had some difficulty in grasping the nature and meaning of a contract, and that it was almost impossible for them to use the contract realistically against other parties. Some parents also felt that the contract was imposed on them, in spite of their participation.

Stein and Gambrill (1976) suggest a two-part foster care contract. The first part of the agreement, they suggest, should be broad, and the second part more precise. Items covered in the first part could include:

- the reason why the placement has been considered;
- the objective of the placement, i.e. what the plan is;
- broad aims within the placement, i.e. provision of good care, being inclusive of the natural family;
- a statement concerning the potential consequences of non-compliance or non-participation by the parties;
- the time limits for the placement;
- a statement defining the broad roles, rights and obligations of each party to the agreement. If necessary, this can include statements about what is not expected.

- a broad statement to the effect that this is a team enterprise and that the parties agree to work co-operatively, and
- provision for how any disputes or disagreements concerning the guidelines or their interpretation are to be handled.

These broad guidelines, with some modifications, will appear in most contracts. It is the specific guidelines with each party that will mostly provide the needed direction (see Shaw & Hipgrave, 1983).

(a) The Child/Foster Parent Contract

Sheldon (1986) gave the following example, inserted as part of a contract between the foster carers and an adolescent:

> The foster parents, Mr. and Mrs. . . . agree that if John returns home by 10.00 p.m. on weekdays and 10.45 p.m. on Saturdays, nothing will be said to him about where he has been going or what he has been doing. If John is late, they will ensure that he forfeits time the next night.
>
> John agrees that in exchange for the privilege of being allowed out late he will:
> (a) try hard to keep on time;
> (b) forfeit double time for each five-minute period he is late without an acceptable excuse, and twenty minutes for each five-minute period after half an hour has elapsed past the deadline, regardless of excuses. The time will be forfeited on the following night.

(b) The Social Worker/Foster Carer(s) Contract

The contract should also clarify the obligations of the social worker and the agency in relation to the foster carers, i.e.:

- the social worker will visit every fortnight, on such-and-such a date, unless otherwise agreed (both foster carers, as far as possible, to be available);
- each visit will review how the placement is progressing and possible difficulties discussed;
- the foster carers will be invited to the reviews and share in any new planning;

- the agency will ensure that the fostering payments are paid on time, as well as clothing and footwear allowances, etc., and
- in the case of a dispute between foster carers and social worker, the matter will be referred to a Principal Officer and perhaps a member of the Foster Carers Association.

(c) The Social Worker/Parent Contract

Besides the broad expectations referred to earlier, the contract has to set out specific expectations, for example in this contract with Mrs Smith:

- Mrs Smith will try to sort out her difficulties and make a home for her child within the next 12 months. Specific improvements will be necessary in her housing circumstances, improved housekeeping and greater stability in her relationships;
- that Mrs Smith accepts the visits of a family-aide to help her with the other children;
- will visit her child on the following days and times: . . . . In the event of any changes, then the foster carers should be given advance warning. Mrs Smith should support the foster carers and the child in their living arrangements. [It is not unusual for parents, who feel aggrieved or 'confused', to seriously disrupt the placement, either intentionally or otherwise.] It is agreed that the parents will also keep in touch with the child by letter and by telephone at least once a week;
- will attend reviews;
- if things go well, Mrs Smith will be allowed, after the first six months, to have the child home for weekends.

As well as setting out specific contract expectations, the two parties will have to negotiate appropriate sanctions. The social worker must also agree to fulfil specific expectations from the parent. For example:

The social worker, Miss Kelly, undertakes:

- to assist Mrs Smith to secure better accommodation, and to sort out her personal problems. Miss Kelly will also write to the Housing Department supporting Mrs Smith's application to be re-housed;

- Miss Kelly will be visiting every week and more frequently if agreed by both parties. The date of the visit will be . . . ;
- Miss Kelly will provide a home-aide;
- for the first month of the placement, Miss Kelly will take Mrs Smith to see her child in the foster home, and
- in the case of a dispute, the matter would be referred to . . .

(d) The Contract with the Child

The contract with the child must be clear about expectations, particularly in terms of rules and certain behaviour. To avoid the danger of this being seen as a negative approach, it is useful to start first with the objectives and time-limits of the placement. Too many 'don'ts' can be off-putting and counter-productive. Inevitably, however, children must know where they stand about certain things. Select the kind of behaviour around which change is being sought, and set out how this is going to be achieved. It is useful to spell out any specific rules, e.g.:

- no smoking in one's bedroom;
- the taking of drugs is unacceptable;
- attend school regularly;
- the possibility of visiting home after some time can be written in;
- write or phone parents once a week;
- attend reviews and share in planning about the future;
- raise with the social worker any issues that cannot be resolved between themselves and the foster carers; and
- amount of pocket-money per week to be specified.

This kind of contract-making will depend on the child's age, the reasons for being in foster care and the circumstances of their natural family. Some children will be too young to participate in any such contracts, others may present too many behaviour problems.

Shaw and Hipgrave (1983) point out that terms in the contract 'which have not been the object of genuine consensus, are likely to be ignored or dismissed by parties even if they have signed. On the other hand, for many people, a genuine verbal promise is a sufficient bond and not enhanced by the attachment of an autograph',

(p. 111). More important, in our view, is the regular review of how the agreement is going, and never to assume that because something has been written in the contract, it has necessarily been fully understood or that there will be no lapses requiring renegotiation. The contract is a useful tool for providing purposefulness and clarifying some of the complexities of fostering, but it is not a substitute for the detailed and sensitive work that is required all round.

KEY POINTS FOR PRACTICE

- The social worker in foster care is involved in complex working relationships with at least three other parties i.e., the child, the parents and the foster carers. The complexity of these relationships can easily lead to misperceptions and ambiguities.

- Empirically-based evidence suggests that the stability of the placement can be threatened through failure to clarify roles and expectations.

- The idea of a contract between the different parties can help give direction to the arrangements by outlining the role and tasks of each party. The success of the contractual arrangements can itself depend on regular feedback and reviews.

3   Recruiting and Training Foster Carers

The search for ways to attract more foster carers is not a preoccupation of the United Kingdom alone, but also of many other countries. It has been so for a very long time. Most agencies embark upon recruitment campaigns because they always require more foster carers. On the other hand, the idea of training for foster carers is of a more recent origin and its provision is far from widespread.

RECRUITMENT

Recruitment is inevitably linked to motivation and what particularly attracts families to take in someone else's child. Motives, like children's needs, are complex, and can vary and change. Fanshel (1966) nearly thirty years ago claimed to have found from his research, that any one or a combination of the following could act as motivating factors: the need on the part of the mother to 'undo' parental deprivations (no reference is made to fathers); identification with the underdog; putting religious beliefs in action, and enjoying the challenge of a difficult job and financial incentive. The only motive that Fanshel found to be 'pathogenic' was the foster mother's perception of herself as a 'benefactress' of children. Apparently mothers with deprived childhoods did not show the same pathogenic tendencies. This is supported by Dando and Minty's (1987) more recent British study.

The possibility that those fostering may expect some form of conscious or unconscious satisfaction from undertaking this task is not necessarily 'pathogenic', provided it is not the exclusive motive. Depending on the context, it would possibly be more worrying had the foster carers not expected some benefits or rewards. Kline and Overstreet (1972) rightly point out that the choice of foster parenthood is usually an expression of varying degrees of the 'mature capacity for parenthood' and the capacity and need to give love which equally can be accompanied by a variety of neurotic motives of varying degrees of severity. The task of selectors, as they add, is to distinguish between 'healthy' and 'neurotic' motives and their extent, and to try to anticipate their possible effect on a particular child.

Paying foster carers

The possibility of a financial incentive as a motive to foster has attracted much attention over the years. In a previous chapter it was noted that the tradition developed over many centuries, that fostering was something that families (meaning mostly women) took on out of kindness and sheer altruism and with no financial compensation or reward in mind. As a result, families who were content with the minimum allowance, or better still, no allowance at all, were viewed as particularly suitable. The opposite was true of those who questioned the level of the allowance. The widespread feeling, including the official view, was that the boarding-out allowance should not have any element of reward for fear of attracting the wrong people. Fears of 'baby farming' (a legacy of the second part of the 19th century) added to the discouragement of any reward reflected in the allowance.

The introduction of specialist fostering with its emphasis on professionalism and the payment of fees for a job done, has contributed to a radical rethink of the policy on pay. The success, also, of adoption allowance schemes introduced in 1983 was to erode further the argument that love and money could not go together (Hill *et al.*, 1989). It would also be a very unusual foster carer who did not consider the question of rewards in a society whose emphasis is on allowing market forces to determine the value of goods and services.

The Children Act 1989 introduced a new and possibly unintentional twist to the notion of payment. The requirement of the Act that authorities should first look for foster placements for children among the child's own extended family, has resulted in children 'being literally dumped on relatives with no assessment, support or fostering allowance' (Rickford, 1992).

What about the attitudes of the foster children and their carers to the payment of allowances or fees? Triseliotis (1980) posed these questions first to children who had grown up in long-term foster care and then to the carers themselves. The children, who were aged 21 at the time of enquiry, far from feeling resentful that their foster carers had been paid to look after them, were critical of 'the authorities' for paying totally inadequate allowances. Many commented that their foster parents made personal sacrifices on their behalf something the children felt their carers shouldn't have had to do. More recently the debate in the UK has shifted not to whether foster carers should get a reward out of fostering, but whether this should be restricted only to those taking in children with special needs, particularly adolescents displaying emotional and behavioural difficulties, or to cover all foster carers. Denmark has been paying all its foster carers a salary since 1970 (Southon, 1986).

On present evidence the relationship between recruitment of foster carers and levels of rewards is still tenuous. However, there is accumulating evidence pointing to the scarcity of foster placements, particularly for adolescents and teenagers. Many children have often to wait for long periods before suitable placements can be found and sometimes they never are. For example, in their study Shaw and Hipgrave (1989b) highlight the scarcity of foster carers with the necessary skills to take on specific tasks. Similar findings were reported by a survey carried out by *Social Work Today* (24.9.92).

A representative of the National Foster Care Association (NFCA), Pat Verity, has said that a growing number of foster carers were deciding to stop and that the situation was getting worse throughout Britain. She attributed this to four reasons: the low level of allowances paid by some authorities; the expectation of much more contact between children and their families under the Children Act 1989; the fear of being accused of abusing a child, and the pressure on social services budgets plus increased work loads from new legislation leading to some authorities cutting back on support for foster carers (Verity, 1988). Campbell and Whitelaw-Downs (1987) claim to have found that higher allowances resulted in a greater proportion of approved families who proceeded to take children. An American study (Chamberlain *et al.*, 1992) has found that the drop-out rate of foster carers is significantly reduced when they are better paid, better trained and better supported by the agency.

The published figures by the Department of Health and a number of studies show how over the years the number of foster carers has not increased significantly. What has mostly changed is the higher percentage of children who are now fostered compared to the past, mainly because of the decrease in the overall number of children in care. For example, in 1980 there were 100,200 children in care in England and Wales of whom almost 37,000 (or 36 per cent) were boarded out. In 1991 there were just under 60,000 children in care of whom 34,300 (57 per cent) were boarded out. Going further back to 1966, the number of children in care then was 67,000 and those in foster care 35,000 (52 per cent). The Scottish pattern follows closely that for England and Wales.

Bebbington and Miles (1990) who studied the characteristics of 2,694 foster homes in England and compared them with representative families from the 1985 General Household survey found that foster families typically include a woman in the 31–55 age group. Also that they tend to live in homes with three or more bedrooms, are two-parent families with one parent working full-time and the other not and that they have older children only. In their survey, five per cent of foster families were non-white approximating the percentage in the general population. (The same writers also found that in 1989 eleven per cent of children coming into care were non-white, of whom six per cent were of mixed race.) The same authors also found no differences in characteristics between those undertaking different types of fostering. Their suggestions for improving local authority recruitment include better reward, better support and the acceptance of a greater proportion of applicants. In fact increased support to retain existing carers seems preferable to continued new recruitment.

While the relationship between levels of fees and recruitment may have not yet been fully established, the big discrepancies between agencies found by Rickford (1992) could be viewed as disquieting. For example, one authority in London paid £285 a week per child while a Welsh one paid only £89 for similar schemes. The same study reports other wide discrepancies, this time between mainstream fostering schemes. Maclean (1989), commenting that in Bradford only 10–20 per cent of the placements were not fee-paying, added that among other things, the payment of fees offered 'equal opportunities for one of the most exploited groups in our society: carers' (p. 29). We were not told how Bradford's move affected the recruitment of black foster carers.

Shaw and Hipgrave (1989a) found from their survey that the idea of same-race placement was widely accepted, at least in specialist fostering. In fact, some authorities were in the unusual position of having on their books black or Asian carers but not enough black or Asian children to place with them. They then raise the question of whether 'it is ever appropriate to use black carers for white children, not least as some agencies are finding it easier to recruit black than white carers' (p. 16).

Recruitment Campaigns

There are many different ways of publicizing the need for foster carers, and most fostering agencies use at least some of these: local and national newspapers; radio and television; the delivery of leaflets to people's homes; setting up market stalls for publicity purposes, and the placing of posters in health centres and hospitals, in churches, temples, mosques and synagogues, on buses, trains and in private cars.

Whatever the choice of publicity, however, there is a need throughout to keep two main issues in mind. First, it is important to give a clear message regarding the fostering task: What kinds of foster carers are being looked for? What are they being required to do? What ages of children require fostering? Too many agencies produce vague and overtly sentimental material, which often proves counter-productive. Secondly, it is crucial to use limited staff and financial resources wisely.

Material needs to be eye-catching and realistic. Many fostering agencies use photographs of children. Those which use photographs of foster carers seem often successful at projecting the image of the kinds of people who may otherwise consider themselves to be unsuitable. Often these are just the kinds of people who are desperately needed by fostering agencies, for example, people who are black, single and older. At this initial stage in the recruitment process opportunity should be taken to target particular people by the use of visual images, the black press and institutions, or by selecting a particular neighbourhood or housing estate in order to attract working-class and local people. Most agencies require foster carers who live within easy contact of children's families and within reach of their schools and friends. For example, in a campaign one of the authors managed in a West London local authority, 11,000 households were targeted, each receiving a leaflet detailing requirements for foster carers. The leaflet was inserted in a local free newspaper, so delivery was taken care of by the newspaper itself. Also the previous week's publication included an article describing the fostering task and the need for foster carers locally, and informing people that the following week they would receive a leaflet detailing all of this.

In order not to lose these potential recruits, social workers need to respond quickly. They need to be at the end of a telephone. The most effective response is an informal meeting where people are invited to talk to social workers, who will explain the role and tasks of fostering. The active involvement of existing fosterers is always of great value. It is vital that enquirers are given full information at an early stage, so that potential foster carers can then decide whether or not fostering is for them. Many will drop out at this stage after they have learned that fostering other people's children is not the same as raising their own children or adoption; that it involves caring for often distressed and demanding children, regularly meeting the children's own parents and other relatives, and working closely with social workers and other staff. Many people often withdraw when they learn that they have to work towards returning children home to their own families. By this stage agencies should have a group of better informed recruits who will be ready to apply formally to become foster carers. They will need to know what happens next and what will be expected of them. Depending on agency policy, applicants will be asked to take part first in training sessions, before individual assessment starts. Other agencies may prefer to have both training and assessment proceeding simultaneously.

TRAINING FOSTER CARERS

The Department of Health's guide to foster care practice (1976) devotes two chapters (and parts of others) to the assessment and selection process, but only two or three references to the usefulness of 'discussion groups' both for applicants and for existing carers. Training in any structured, formal sense is not described at all. It is referred to as a possibility for those who are carrying out particularly skilled fostering tasks such as caring for older children with very disturbed backgrounds, but they clearly do not see this as a universal requirement.

The move towards viewing training and preparation as necessary for foster carers came mainly after the 1970s with the introduction into the UK of professional fostering schemes, particularly those geared towards fostering adolescents. It was gradually becoming apparent that foster carers could not be expected to undertake such demanding tasks without preparation, training, post-placement support and continued training. This new appreciation of the task also led to many Social Services Departments and voluntary agencies establishing specialist social work teams under a variety of names: 'Home Finding', 'Fostering and Adoption', 'Family Placement', 'Child Resource', etc. These brought together specialist workers in groups. Prior to that, many fostering specialists had either worked as part of a generic social work team, or even had fostering as only a small part of a generic workload. Specialist teams had the resources and the specific focus to develop fostering practice, particularly training. Over time the training ethos from specialist schemes spread wider into the more traditional mainstream areas of fostering. Research by the Foster Care Steering Group of the Care Sector Consortium, published in 1992, showed that training was offered to most foster carers as part of their approval process. Sadly they also noted that training opportunities were less available to foster carers after they had been approved. However, the same group also reported that 'the content of the training is determined locally and is variable in quality and quantity' (Paras 3–4).

Why Training

The 'Guidance and Regulations in Family Placements' acknowledges that 'fostering is more and more recognized as a skilled task, needing training and support and foster parents have an important role in the professional team concerned with a child's care' (Department of Health, 1990, p. 22). Triseliotis (1989) in his summary of foster care outcomes, cites a number of studies which found that carers who are prepared, trained and supported are more likely to succeed. Other findings such as those which point to higher levels of disruption for older children and/or children who display emotional and behavioural difficulties, or that children who experience consistent parental contact are found to be more stable and settled in their foster care placements, point to the need for foster carers to have appropriate training to understand more about the task and why certain practices are pursued. Better training for foster carers will empower them to negotiate, debate and sometimes stand up to other professionals and managers from a position of greater equality.

Research not only highlights the areas in which training may be particularly important. It can also tell us something about the effectiveness of specific types of training. Hampston and Tavormina (1980) studied the relative effectiveness of two different approaches to group training for foster mothers. They found that a behavioural approach was more effective in helping them reduce children's behaviour difficulties. On the other hand a reflective approach helped the foster carers to have a more positive view of the child's own parents. Cautley's research also suggests that foster fathers in particular respond positively to explicit suggestions with regard to handling behaviour – a finding which would suggest that they would respond to a behavioural approach.

Designing a Training Programme

As has already been said, fostering is a complex task. Training for it draws on people's desire to care for children and/or young people, and their current child-rearing ideas and skills. One of the hurdles a training programme must overcome is the possibility that would-be foster carers may have a false impression about the fostering task, what it entails, and their capacity to carry it out. A course of training therefore needs to act as a preparation for the reality of the task. This can act as a 'final sieve' in the self-selection aspect of the approval process – the applicant is now in a more informed position when making a realistic decision as to whether or not they can commit themselves to the varied demands of the fostering task.

Having stayed committed (or become even more committed), as people continue with the training and assessment process, and the task is more clearly understood, a secondary objective then comes to the fore. Agency workers want prospective carers not only to know what they may face in practice, important as that is, but also to be able to do it well! Doing the task well requires more than pure commitment, it also requires knowledge and skills. Knowledge and skills, combined with commitment, are more likely to lead to carers being successful, and hence finding the task rewarding.

This purpose can best be achieved by affirming, through the approach to training, that people already begin with ideas, skills, experiences with children, situations and organizations, and have developed strategies for coping with problems. These should be taken account of and drawn upon as the course leaders introduce conceptual frameworks from the field of child care and some key ideas and techniques for managing the child in placement, working with the child's family and the agency, and whatever other themes and topics have been built into the course design.

To design and organize a training programme for foster carers a number of questions require answers:

- What do foster carers need to know?
- What is it possible to put into a basic programme?
- What teaching methods will be appropriate and effective?
- What materials will promote understanding and enhance and maintain the participants' interest?
- What organizational issues need to be taken into account?

What do Foster Carers need to know?

A review of the subject matter of general foster carer training courses produces a broad consensus with regard to content. No doubt each course design will have its own emphasis and special topics, but a selection of the following list of topics will very likely be at the core of them all:

- Child development
- The causes of low self-esteem/building self-esteem
- Attachment theory
- Socialization and/or institutionalization
- The effects of separation and loss
- Managing difficult behaviour
- The child care system

- Working and planning as part of a team
- The role of social workers
- The role and significance of the child's parents and origins, including the importance of racial and ethnic identity
- The role of the foster carers
- Attitudes and awareness with regard to issues such as race, gender and disability
- The impact of fostering on the foster family
- Awareness with regard to child sexual abuse (knowledge of signs and symptoms, how to make placements safe for the child and the family, handling disclosures, etc.)
- HIV and AIDS.

A balance will have to be struck between what topics are appropriate, at what level during the pre-assessment/selection period are they introduced, and what could be part of continuing training. While many fostering agencies will have devised their own training packs covering a range of such topics, the most widely used training packs will be those which can be bought. These are the National Foster Care Association's (NFCA) successor to 'Parenting Plus', an eight two-hour session course entitled 'The Challenge of Foster Care', and the Open University course 'Caring for Children and Young People'. A summary of the sessions involved demonstrates the scope of the training on offer.

What is Possible to Put Onto a Basic Programme?

The Challenge of Foster Care's eight sessions deal mainly with the fostering task as follows:

Session 1. Setting the scene: Who needs fostering?
            Why do children come into care?
            What are foster carers trying to offer?
Session 2. Being well prepared – getting ready for the job.
Session 3   Working together with children, parents and social workers, and the importance of information-sharing.
Session 4. Dealing with difficult behaviour – the problems of the first few months.
Session 5. Teamwork and decision-making in placements.
Session 6. Developing specialist skills, e.g., an introduction to working with older children.

47

Session 7. Saying goodbye to children – letting go and moving on.

Session 8. Looking back, looking forward – are you ready for the job?

The Open University course 'Caring for Children and Young People' is slightly different in its orientation. It is aimed at 'all those who care for other people's children in social services, health and education', not just foster carers.

The first topic explores what it is like to be an adolescent, and then pursues a number of themes related to adolescence, for example, adolescence as a 'quest for adult identity' and as a phenomenon 'constructed' by society. It then broadens out to look at aspects of child development, identity and self-esteem.

The next topic looks at children and young people in families. It considers what a family is, and how important it is in shaping the child – alongside the powerful influence of social and cultural factors.

In the third session the factors which cause us most stress are considered. It looks at how stress affects feelings and behaviour, and why it is that some families under stress are more at risk than others of 'breaking down'.

The next three topics look at 'The Continuum of Care'. It starts by looking at community support and the family in the community, and how the community can affect whether or not a family in crisis can continue to care for its children. The next topic considers the services – both statutory and voluntary – which are provided to help children, young people and their families in the community. The third topic looks at the process of coming into substitute care, the range of care options, and the task of selecting and managing a successful placement. It highlights the decisions that have to be made, and the practice implications.

The next three sessions look closely at the problems involved in 'Living with Strangers'. It looks at 'transitions', particularly those experienced by young people living with strangers, and how to help them deal with them, particularly given the likelihood of low self-esteem and self-confidence. It looks at the implications for the quality of daily living experience that ought to be provided for them, and for the skills needed by the carers who must provide these experiences. In the final part of this section different types of crisis are considered, and how the behaviour of people in crisis stems from their level of self-esteem, and how crises can themselves have a powerful input on self-esteem. Finally it considers some techniques and strategies for dealing constructively with crisis situations.

The last three sessions of the course focus specifically on residential care, and at some of the problems associated with caring for other people's children in residential settings. Despite the emphasis on residential care, some of the issues covered are just as relevant for foster carers – topics such as 'working with other professionals', and 'maintaining children's links with home and neighbourhood'.

The course outlines for 'The Challenge of Foster Care' and the Open University course give us an idea of the range of topics which are felt to be relevant to foster carers, but to design a course we need to go further than simply putting together a list of topics. We need to look beyond a simple list of topics to make clear to ourselves what our basic concerns about fostering are and therefore what our training objectives should be. However, both this and the NFCA's training programmes lack input in early child development theory such as attachment, separation and loss, socialization, identity formation and generally early stages of personality development.

Gray (1992), in her work at the then Derby Fostering and Adoption Unit, and later in her unpublished work at Sheffield University entitled 'History, Development and Reception of a Programme of Training for Those Involved in Substitute Care', produced a list of statements of concern and a related array of course objectives. Slightly adapted, her concerns were:

1. Fostering is more than parenting. It includes natural parents, and a rehabilitative function. Consequently carers will need to be aware of the role of the child's own parents in the child's life, helped to be more aware of their task as 'substitute parents' and the impact of rehabilitation on themselves.

2. Living in another family is not 'natural' in this society and leads to difficulties in feelings for all those concerned. The impact of rejection and the problems it may cause need to be understood and prepared for.

3. Taking in a 'stranger' means that everyone will have to adjust. The prospective foster family can be helped to use techniques for

forecasting the likely impact that a foster child will have on their family.

4. Families in crisis may fail or need temporary support. Blame is unhelpful. Carers need to be helped to understand how parents feel.

5. When agencies take over from parents, life-planning is essential because the natural course of events has been interrupted. Carers need an appropriate level of awareness about planning for children and the issues and difficulties facing decision-makers. This should lead on to an introduction to placement plans and the need for placement goals to fit in with the long-terms aims of the agency for the child.

6. Some experiences adversely affect children and young people's development in social, emotional, moral and psychological terms. Carers therefore need to have a basic understanding of child development, and of how children become social beings through the process of socialization. They need to be clear that experience affects development, and to be familiar with the effects of a range of experiences common amongst the children that they are likely to be looking after, such as the effects of separation from, and loss of, their family of origin, the effects of rejection, prejudice and physical and sexual abuse.

7. Some experiences adversely affect a child's self-concept. Carers need to understand something of how the concept of self develops, and how it is affected by experiences such as those listed in previous paragraphs.

8. Experience shapes behaviour, which is an outward sign of adjustment/maladjustment. Regression needs to be understood as one behavioural outcome of unsatisfactory development. Carers need to be helped to understand that their observations of behaviour can help the team involved reach an understanding of the experiences that have created that behaviour. Experience may be shaped by race, gender and/or disability.

9. The child is a product of an environmental system, and this needs to be considered when care and treatment are decided.

10. Re-shaping of behaviour involves an analysis of the problem and the development of a plan of treatment. Carers need to know, in general terms, what the management of behaviour involves. The basic rules of behaviour modification are a useful and practical example of behaviour management.

11. Children need to understand their history and experiences in order to come to terms with them. Carers need to understand how a child feels when the State intervenes in their family life, and to be introduced to techniques for working with children who have lost a sense of their 'roots', or express a need to understand their past.

12. Treatment may involve sanctions and rewards. Attitude to this treatment needs to be carefully thought through.

13. Each person in an interaction affects the process and out-come. Carers need to focus on themselves in order to raise their awareness of the effect that they may have on those with whom they interact.

14. Prejudice and stereotyping restrict the lives of children and young people and affect their development, self-concept and behaviour. Carers need to be helped to be aware of racism and sexism, and issues concerning attitudes towards disability and sexual orientation.

15. All carers need to be aware of the significant possibility that the children and young people with whom they work may have been subject to sexual abuse, whether or not this is known prior to placement. Carers will therefore need to know about the signs and symptoms which may indicate sexual abuse and how to respond to a child telling them about what has happened. They will need to know about the agency's procedures and their role in them. Furthermore they will need to give some thought as to how to manage their household in such a way that it helps the foster child to feel safe, minimizes the risk of further abuse occurring, and helps the whole family feel, and be, safe.

16. All carers also need to be aware that they, their family members and their foster child may have been exposed to the risk of HIV and AIDS. Issues around the infection and how it is spread need to be discussed so that carers can manage their house-holds with the necessary hygiene standards, provide appropriate education for their foster child, and provide a supportive service for children and families living with HIV and AIDS.

This can appear a daunting – and yet probably incomplete – set of objectives for a foster care training programme. In reality, trainers will be working within time constraints and with limited resources at hand, and will inevitably have to make decisions about priorities and emphases, about what might be described as 'core material' and what is more peripheral, as well as what approach, or combination of approaches to take.

As early as 1979 Passmark identified two basic kinds of training. One she called 'the broad spectrum approach'; the other 'specialized aspects of foster parenting'. These resonate with Brown's (1988) later study of the effects of two foster parent training methods on the attitudes of foster carers. He called these the 'skills' approach, which used structured teaching time with an explicit emphasis on building the carers' skills, and the 'issues' approach, which means essentially an open discussion approach. He found that the skills approach was the more effective; it offered more help with a larger percentage of the foster parents' self-reported problems than did the issues training. He recommends that a successful curriculum combines some of each of these approaches as each has its benefits. The one affords applicants a broad perspective on the fostering task as part of the child care resource, while the other offers specific skills which should enable foster carers to carry out their work in caring for and managing children, and working with their families and the agency.

Training Methods, Materials and Organizational Issues

Having established aims and approach, a number of principles need to be considered in constructing a course. Adult learners are already in possession of many conceptual structures. In terms of care, management, growth and development of children, the social problems of families in crisis, and the statutory responsibility of local government and relationships between people, adults come to a training course with, between them, a great deal of experience, knowledge and insight. A course for adult learners, therefore, needs to draw on the knowledge they bring and fit it into framework, or, as Lowell (1980) says 'provide a scaffolding of ideas to bridge the gap between what the student knows already and what he needs to know before he can learn the new material in a meaningful fashion' (p. 141).

An example of this might be the teaching of aspects of child development. Most course members will come with some knowledge of their own. Some explanation, exercises and discussion around a particular theoretical approach, for example, Erikson's theory of child development, will allow people to become aware of their own child-rearing experiences, or of their observations of children, and fit these constructively into a framework for understanding development trends, outcomes, problems, etc. It can then be used to enhance their practice by helping them to understand that the developmental outcomes for a child may be alleviated by new and healing here-and-now experiences.

Theories such as Erikson's need to be introduced to foster carers because they are theories that practitioners have found useful in understanding how children develop. Carers need not just understand why children are behaving and feeling the way that they do, they also need some means of responding to such behaviour and feelings in a way that will enhance the child's growth and development. Exercises and experiences offered in the training can provide carers with opportunities to 'rehearse' or plan how they are going to apply their learning in their day-to-day work as foster carers. It is important that the material presented must be at an appropriate level, near the edge of the participants' experience. Gray (1992) also recommends moving from fundamental theoretical concepts with only a small proportion of each session related to practice issues, to more and more practice-related sessions.

When teaching adults it is important that they are treated with respect, and as prospective colleagues who are engaged in mutual enquiry with the course leaders. There needs to be recognition that many course members will not be academically oriented, and may have had unhappy or unsatisfactory school experiences which may have created a negative attitude towards learning. Consequently, comfortable, non-threatening methods should be used in the early stages. Similarly, not all applicants will be equally motivated, and interest levels will vary. As a result, methods should be geared to adult interests and abilities, and should be varied. The introduction of experiential and group-oriented methods should probably be introduced gradually. Attention must be paid to achieving a balance of active and passive learning.

Adult learners are generally believed to learn better if they plan their own learning (Knowles, 1970). However, this is not realistic for prospective entrants to a new area of work. The course designer and leaders therefore have to take responsibility for deciding what the participants need to know and to think about before starting to foster. The leader has to accept the role of organizer, facilitator and provider of material. (Experienced foster carers are of course in a much better position to choose appropriate further learning. Training also can draw on their experience and expertise by involving them from the start in joint planning).

The specific teaching techniques used can be combined. There can be elements of direct teaching and discursive elements, including more active and experiential learning. There may be readings to reinforce what has been taught, or to prepare for the session to come. Video or audio tapes may have the same role. Group participants may be asked to observe and perhaps record some activity, or practise some skill between sessions. Variety is important. Both active and passive learning skills are required of the group. Groups listen, read, discuss in small or large settings, analyse material, respond to – and ask – questions, use diagrams, work on problems and perform role plays. They may be asked for quick and immediate responses, or to give considered responses after a period of study.

In their choice of method and technique, leaders also need to take into account that some of the material, for example that relating to the sexual abuse of children, or rejection, may be very emotionally demanding and distressing. The course needs to be balanced so that it can be emotionally powerful without becoming a stressful ordeal. A good basic training programme stimulates its trainees, and gives them a positive attitude towards further training. As they gain more and more experience they can specify their own training needs and contribute to the training of others.

Post-approval Training and Special Topics

Post-approval training can build on areas already covered in initial training and also bring in new topics which were either too narrow in their focus to be part of the initial training or which the carers now themselves feel would be of use to them. Though no doubt this list could be expanded, potential topics would include:

- Working with sexually-abused children
- Equal opportunities in foster care
- Working with the child's natural family
- The law and foster care
- HIV and AIDS
- Managing challenging behaviour

- Life story book work
- Specific kinds of fostering: adolescents, remand, children with disabilities, etc.
- Preparing children for placement
- Communicating with children
- Approaches to therapy.

The British Agencies for Adoption and Fostering (BAAF) and the NFCA have both taken significant steps in providing an 'off-the-peg' post-approval training programme aimed at enhancing the abilities of carers.

The NFCA's course, 'A Problem Shared: A Practical Approach to Difficult Foster Placements' is aimed at practising foster carers, and their social workers. The course aims to enable participants to manage difficult behaviour in a systematic way and to view the child's behaviour in a context and as a whole. It also aims to reinforce the importance of teamwork, and the fostering task, as well as helping participants to identify their skills and those that they need to develop. The BAAF course 'In Touch with Children' is a five-day course aimed, specifically, at developing skills in communicating with, and assessing, children.

Alongside these very general, and valuable, courses the major areas of training development and concern in recent years have been around race and the impact of racism, working with sexually-abused children and young people, and most recently, an increasing awareness of the need to prepare carers for work involving children living with HIV and AIDS. In our experience, such issues are usually first considered as specialist topics, primarily as training for staff and experienced carers, before being absorbed – at least to some degree – into the initial training programme.

Race Issues in Foster Care Training

As late as 1979, even in the US, Passmark (1979) could write about the absence of any specific training on what she calls 'those competencies related to fostering racial or cultural minority children and helping a child maintain identity through appropriate cultural and familial ties'. The first stumbling steps into this area, which were made prior to the development and promotion of 'same-race' placement policies, were primarily practical guides for white carers looking after black children. Hair care, skin care, dietary issues and religious practices were the themes. Self-awareness, anti-discriminatory practices, and understanding racism, and the impact it has on the lives of young people were not the order of the day.

Increasingly the social work profession has recognized that the needs of black children are best met within black families. One of the implications of the policy change arising from this is that training on race issues is no longer based on the assumption that carers are white, nor that the issues around transracial placements are simply practical ones (not that these areas should be neglected if transracial placements occur).

There would be wide agreement now that all training material should be multicultural (as, for example, the NFCA's 'A Problem Shared'), and that basic training should promote anti-discriminatory and anti-racist practices as well as educating carers, both black and white, about the impact of racism on the sense of identity and self-esteem of young people growing up in a racist society. There has been a risk that the implementation of 'same-race' policies could have lead to a belief that training in these areas was no longer necessary because black carers would somehow be expected to know all that was needed. In reality, this is a subtle and complex area of work and training remains important. In a separate development, Almas (1992) has questioned the appropriateness of training Asian and white foster carers together. He argues that for reasons of language, knowledge of fostering and cultural and religious reasons there is a case for separate training courses. However, pragmatic considerations may override these arguments in many areas.

Working with Children who have been Sexually Abused

Increasing awareness of the sexual abuse of children and young people has had major implications for foster care workers:

> Sometimes it is only within the security of a foster or adoptive home that children may feel able to divulge such sensitive secrets from their past. It is, therefore, essential that every substitute family is knowledgeable about the reality of sexual abuse, sensitive to its implications and aware that they may find themselves unexpectedly parenting a sexually abused child.

> Training in child sexual abuse for foster and adoptive families is not an optional extra: it is crucial. (MacCaskill, 1991, p. 113)

MacCaskill (1991) came to this conclusion on the basis of her study of 66 adoptive and foster families caring for children who had been abused. She found that there were evident disadvantages for families undertaking this task without training. She found that parenting was being undertaken in an unconfident manner, and opportunities were sometimes missed for enabling children to talk about their personal experiences of abuse because the carers had not grasped the importance of disclosure. Inappropriate sexualized behaviour was sometimes reinforced because of the carers' lack of knowledge and preparation for the intrusive and disruptive influence that an abused child could have on family life which became a factor in some placement disruptions. Some families put themselves at risk of being the subject of allegations of abuse because they were unaware of their vulnerability.

MacCaskill was clearly not alone in her concerns. Already specialist courses had been developed. For example McFadden (1986) in the US produced her training course 'Fostering The Child Who Has Been Sexually Abused' in 1986. A year later Barnardo's North East produced 'A Child Sexual Abuse Training Programme for Foster Parents with Teenage Placements' (Davis *et al.*, 1987).

The range of topics covered by the courses cited above match fairly closely with the issues that carers themselves indicated should be included in training in MacCaskill's research, and fall into the following categories:

1. Facts and Information
   Causes/origins, incidence and etiology of abuse.
   Physical and behavioural signs and symptoms of abuse.
   The effects of abuse, short and long-term.
   What is known about offenders.
   Definitions of sexual abuse.
   The victim's feelings.
2. Disclosure Work
   How to enable and support disclosure by the child.
   How to respond to disclosure.
   Procedures following on from disclosure.
3. Coping with the range of behaviour difficulties that may arise

with sexually abused children: from sexually inappropriate behaviour to self-harming.

4. The effects on the foster family.

> Keeping the family and the child safe.
>
> Changes to family life-style.
>
> Stress on marriages and on the foster carer's own children.

5. Therapies

> Kinds of therapy available.
>
> The role of the foster carers in carrying out and/or supporting therapy.

6. Allegations against carers.

> The possibility of allegations.
>
> Explanation of agency procedures in the event of allegations.

7. The carer's own feelings about abuse and sexuality.

8. The importance of teamwork, and the role of the various team members.

McFadden highlights the fact that consideration needs to be given to teaching methods and techniques in running such a course. In many other kinds of training for foster carers, self-disclosure and experiential learning are valuable. But this course contains sensitive and emotive subject matter and some members of the course may themselves have been abused and may only recognize that during the training sessions. Consequently those techniques may be of limited value. She concludes that 'with the intensity of emotion engendered by these issues, it is important for the instructor to provide adequate structure in the sessions to keep the focus on helping the child' (p. 13).

As a final comment, it is important that it is recognized that dealing with the aftermath of sexual abuse is not 'women's work'. It is very important that male carers attend training and give considerable thought to the role that they have to play.

HIV, AIDS and Foster Care

HIV infection is making a significant impact on the foster care service in a number of ways, each of which has training implications.

It is important that all carers are aware that any child who is placed with them may be infected with HIV. This may not be known to the agency placing the child. Early responses, for example the National Foster Care Association (1990b), stressed good hygiene standards and confidentiality issues, alongside information about causation. But with increasing experience in the UK and the USA, approaches are becoming more sophisticated. The Department of Health in 'Children and HIV: Guidance for Local Authorities' (1992), outlines a basic training programme for all carers. It proposes that training should cover:

1. Basic information on HIV and AIDS, including transmission and prognosis.
2. Consideration of the impact of caring for children with HIV at home.
3. Health and safety practices. The guide gives very clear recommendations on hygiene procedures, covering accidents involving blood, cleaning and disposal of waste, as well as good hygiene practices.
4. Confidentiality.
5. Issues around caring for a child facing severe illness and death.
6. Stigma and discrimination.

In addition, all foster carers have some responsibility for sex education, which of course will involve HIV and AIDS, the need for responsibility in sexual relationships and safer sex. Carers may well benefit from support and training to carry out this task effectively.

The training needs of those who choose to care for children known to be HIV-infected, or those who are looking after a child whose HIV status is discovered during the placement will be rather more extensive. So will those who are caring for children who, although not infected themselves, are affected by the presence of HIV in their natural family.

Those caring for HIV-infected children will need substantial training and support to cope with the prospect of caring for a seriously ill child who may die while in their care. Training will help them promote the child's physical health and emotional well-being as well as preparing them for the emotional stress and stigma that they will be working with.

Some, as described by Taylor-Brown (1991), will be working in close partnership with parents who are known to be HIV-positive, providing flexible support as and when needed by the ill parent, and this too will require special training – not just in working with the family, but also in helping their foster child cope with the loss of their parent.

No doubt as practice continues to develop, training will need to be continually reviewed and updated. Finally, foster carers will also have to be prepared for the specific child that is to join them.

4   Assessing Foster Carers

INTRODUCTION

A large part of a social worker's time is usually taken up in collecting information about people in their different situations and circumstances. Based on this, interpretations are then made and decisions taken. Inevitably questions are being asked about the accuracy of such assessments and their possible biases. Nowhere else are such questions being asked with greater persistency than in the assessment of would-be adopters or foster carers. Words such as 'screening' and 'vetting' used in the past to describe this assessment process acquired many negative connotations. Since then ways have been sought to make the process of assessment less intrusive, less subjective and fairer to applicants.

A key factor in generating discontent was the perceived power of social workers in accepting or rejecting applicants. Since then agencies have been looking for ways to make assessment more of a shared process with applicants. Davis et al. (1984) add that the unequal power relationship between social workers and applicants may encourage the development of 'a relationship of dependence', rather than the kind of open partnership which they feel is required in fostering today. They also argue that this approach can create such anxiety and resentment within applicants, that they are not able to take full advantage of the preparation and training that is seen as fundamental to successful fostering.

It is further argued that a move towards a more equal assessment process also creates the atmosphere within which future working relationships with foster carers can be built upon. The new approach, developed over the last couple of decades, usually combines a mixture of individual and group methods which are used to convey information, provide training and finally engage applicants in the process of self-assessment. Shaw (1985), drawing from his review of the literature on foster care selection during the 1970s and 1980s, writes:

> The period under review shows a marked shift in the approach adopted by agencies towards prospective foster parents, from one characterised by detailed scrutiny of their personal history, attitudes and motives to a more open, educational approach to tasks and skills. (p. 50)

Hunter (1989) from a survey of various fostering schemes also found 'a healthy scepticism to traditional vetting'.

We have to recognize that there are no firm criteria of what attributes are required to parent other people's children, who can have diverse needs, temperaments and circumstances. Even when we know what to look for, it is not always easy to recognize it. Interpreting information on such intangibles as motivation, parenting, maturity, stability of couple relationships, warmth and capacity for empathic relationships is far from easy. Much of the criticisms described earlier were attributed to the indiscriminate use of the 'diagnostic' model derived mainly from psychoanalytic theory. By putting most of the emphasis in personality development on the influence of past childhood experiences and on the power of the unconscious to influence motives and behaviour, diagnostic theory possibly led to the adoption of a rather narrow and sometimes perhaps dogmatic approach to assessment. The past is important, but so are also subsequent events, and current interactions and relationships.

The diagnostic model assumed that only those who had 'good' childhood experiences, as defined by theory, would make good foster carers and that the interviewer could recognize 'unhealthy' motives deep in the unconscious of the unknowing applicant(s). The identification of these experiences often meant a detailed investigatory type of interviewing, which, besides the power it conferred on the social worker as 'the expert', paid less attention to social and environmental factors. Psychodynamic theory has made a big contribution to our understanding of human behaviour, but by itself is not enough as an assessment tool for the foster care role. Most of the criticisms for the use of the theory in social work arose, in our view, from the failure to distinguish between insights about personality development and individual behaviour derived from the theory and its clinical application.

It was as a result of this climate of dissatisfaction, that Kirk (1964), with adoptive applicants in mind, offered an alternative approach to assessment and selection by introducing the concept of a group educative approach. The central idea was that following a series of group information/training sessions, those unsuitable for the task would select themselves out. The question of 'vetting' or 'screening' would not, therefore, arise. Though Kirk was over-optimistic about self-selection, nevertheless his ideas have been built on and form the basis of much of present practice. Kirk's educative approach was adapted through the use of ideas from task-centred social work, system models, and methods of adult learning. We shall be returning to these models later in this chapter.

BACKGROUND

Guidelines for the assessment and selection of foster carers existed under the Poor Law, but they were not formalized until after the Children Act 1948. As a result, much of post-World War II foster care work relied until recently on the Boarding-Out Regulations of 1955. These were eventually updated in 1988 and later absorbed, with minor alterations, into the Children Act 1989 Regulations. All the legal requirements and official guidance are now codified in 'The Children Act 1989 Guidance and Regulations, Volume 3, Family Placements'. The regulations clearly accept the concept of approving applicants in respect of 'number and age range of children, or of placements of any particular kind or in any particular circumstance' (Regulation 3 (5)) as well as approval for specific named child or children.

In the 19th century, foster carers had to satisfy Boarding-Out Committees as to their 'moral' character, housing conditions and economic status (DHSS, 1976). While the phrase 'moral character' may be hard to define, there was clearly some concept of personal suitability that the committee were required to consider, as well as health and more practical considerations. In different forms, and in language appropriate to the era, these three aspects of assessment have stayed with us to the present. Schedule 1, of the current Guidance and Regulations, entitled 'Information as to Prospective Parent and Other Members of His Household and Family', lists eleven pieces of information that are required to be obtained 'so far as is practicable'. These include the characteristics of the applicant(s) such as age, accommodation, employment or occupation, standard of living, health, and leisure activities; and interests and details about other members of the household. The schedule also asks about the personality and marital status of the applicant(s), particulars about religious persuasion, racial origin, and cultural and linguistic background. There is also a section about the applicants' previous criminal convictions and those of other members of the household, if any (subject to the Rehabilitation of Offenders Act 1974). Checking criminal convictions could give rise to some resentment (Rhodes, 1992) and social workers need to explain the rationale for these checks. Most people have no difficulty in recognizing how essential these are.

The guidance offered does expand on the list considerably, sometimes explaining why the information is wanted, and suggesting how it can be gathered. From a professional assessment point of view, the most significant perspective added by the guidance is that the assessor should be looking at the applicants' attitudes and expectations around a number of issues that relate to the effective carrying-out of the fostering role. The major ones outlined are applicants' readiness to work with parents as partners and a generally inclusive attitude to the birth family; to provide for the child's physical and emotional needs; to encourage the child's education, and to support the child in achieving their potential and to undertake not to use physical punishment.

The guidance goes on to define corporal punishment and to explain the inappropriateness of using restriction or deprivation of food and drink, or the restriction of contact visits to family and friends, as a form of punishment. It also raises several other assessment issues. It advises social workers to visit at least at a time when they can meet the entire household to explore the relationships of all the members; their degree of participation in the fostering task and the daily life of the foster child, and the demands which they may make on the applicants. Social workers are urged to communicate with the applicants' children to assess their feelings about fostering and to help them and the family think about the impact of fostering on them and their social life. Useful advice is also given on assessing the local amenities (school, transport, etc.), family members who do not live at home, and 'standard of living' and 'life-style', as well as expanding on what it would be useful to know about racial, religious, cultural and linguistic issues.

(This summary of the Guidance is not complete, and is no substitute for reading the 'Guidance and Regulations, Volume 3, Family Placements' itself.)

The aim of gathering all this information is said to be 'to identify all the factors which contribute to a general picture of the applicants, their family and way of life' (Department of Health, 1991, p. 25), but how to interpret that picture is left entirely to the agency. Nor does it indicate which of these factors have been shown by research to correlate with successful or unsuccessful fostering.

Before going on to relate assessment to research findings, we will take a brief look at the kind of assessment processes and procedures that are generally used to meet the requirements of the legislation. The beginning of the assessment procedure is a period in which the agency's primary task is to ensure that the interested enquirer receives sufficient, well-presented, accurate and culturally appropriate information to enable them to make a decision about whether or not they wish to begin the formal application process. Information-giving does not, of course, cease after this stage, but continues throughout the process, during training and beyond. In practice, whatever assessment approach the agency's workers use, the greatest part of the asessment is the applicant's self-assessment.

The information can be given, for example, in the form of 'information evenings', videotapes, home visits by foster care workers, opportunities to meet existing foster carers and/or visit residential establishments, or any combination of these. The presence of experienced foster carers at such meetings to contribute and answer questions, is usually valued by applicants. All studies suggest that having been given initial information, most enquirers make an early decision whether to proceed or not. Others will drop out during the training, assessment and preparation stages. On the basis of what they have heard or learned, many decide that fostering is not for them. Those who decide to proceed are required to name two referees, both of whom must be interviewed. The Guidance and Regulations referred to, state that a referee 'should be someone who is in a position to comment on the applicant's sense of responsibility including his knowledge, understanding and love of children, evidence of sound relationships, his motivation to foster children and his personality' (Department of Health, 1991, p. 27).

The process of assessment usually seems to consist of between five and ten interviews, often a combination of office-based interviews and home visits. In some agencies two workers co-assess the applicants. Some would also like to see a greater involvement of experienced foster carers. The home visits should include at least one to meet the whole household, and would also usually include interviews in which the applicants (if it is a joint application) are seen separately from each other. If there are children in the household, time also needs to be spent with them, with a view to preparing them for the impact that fostering will have, directly and indirectly, on them and assessing their ability and willingness to cope with that impact. With the agreement of the parents, the children may be seen separately.

The current legislation expects a significant number of individual interviews with applicants. Some agencies in the past have endeavoured to use group activities as the focus for assessment. No doubt some will continue to do so, but given the information required now, it is difficult to see that this can be done, except as an addition to a significant number of individual interviews.

TRAINING AND PREPARATION

Introductory training and preparation programmes are often completed during the application process or before. Practices vary. Some agencies also use training as part of the assessment while others keep it separate. Nonetheless many agencies are unwilling to finally approve applicants until they have had at least their initial training. In view of what has been said about the intrusiveness of some selection methods, it may seem fairer to applicants that assessment and selection follow an introductory training programme to enable applicants to understand better the nature of the task.

FINAL APPROVAL PROCESS

In the case of adoption, adoption panels make the final decision, but the guidance and regulations in foster care do not prescribe the final decision-making process, saying that the arrangements 'must reflect the importance of the decision and the need for accountability . . . ' (Department of Health, 1991, p. 28).

However, they clearly lean toward some kind of panel system, including what is described as 'a senior officer designated to make the decision' (p. 29). Whatever decision-making process is used, the agency must give its decisions in writing. A decision to approve an applicant to become a foster carer must also state the terms of approval – that is, whether the approval is solely for a specific child or children, or the number and age ranges of children for whom they are approved, or for specific kinds of placement.

A decision not to approve an application should, as far as is possible, be explained to the applicants. Agencies should provide a representation procedure for reconsideration of their decisions, and to consider an applicant's dissatisfaction with the process itself.

BEYOND LEGAL REQUIREMENTS

So far the emphasis has been on legal requirements and procedures, but there is a lot more to assessment than simply ensuring that these are met. There is much more going on: building working relationships, exchanging information and preparing for the task. Nonetheless, the central task remains for the social worker and the prospective carers to reach a reasoned decision – both separately and together – as to whether the prospective carers and their household and environment are likely to be able to provide a suitable foster home. If so, for what type of fostering task – emergency, respite, short-term remand, medium- or long-term? Within the agreed type of fostering, what type of child (in terms of age, sex, personality, behaviour, etc.) would they be most and least likely to help successfully?

What sort of qualities are to be looked for in an assessment? The range of fostering tasks is now so wide that the answer to that question will vary accordingly. A review of the literature, however, produces a fairly standard range of issues which will no doubt vary in importance according to the particular fostering scheme and the assessment model being employed. The sort of issues raised include a selection of the following, many of which are paraphrased from existing fostering schemes.

Can the carers provide warmth and care without undue need for reciprocation in terms of affection or expectations of the foster child? Will they be able to empathize with the feelings likely to be experienced by the child? To what extent will they be able to accept and handle negative behaviour without rejecting the child? Will they be able to accept and support the child's relationship with its natural family? Will they be able to work in positive partnership with the child's parents? Will they be able to work in partnership with the agency? Will they provide an appropriate standard of physical care? How good will they be at helping troubled children? Do they have sufficient capacity to benefit from training and advice? Do they have sufficient support networks? Will they be able to use support available from the agency and other carers? Will they be able to help children develop a positive view of themselves and their families?

Other questions to be asked or considered include: Are they sufficiently motivated to carry out the demands of the task, and do their motives fit with the task? Are they flexible enough to be able to adapt to the demands of fostering? Are they sufficiently aware of their, and their family system's, strengths and weaknesses? Are they aware that fostering will change their family system? Can they cope with stress, and conflict, and persist in the face of problems and crises? Are they sufficiently aware of the need 'to keep placements safe', i.e., to manage placements in such a way that the risk of abuse, or fear of abuse, is minimized within the foster placement (keeping both the child and themselves safe)? Do their attitudes towards race, gender, disability and sexual orientation meet agency requirements? Can they work within agency policies, for example, on issues of discipline, or smoking? Will they provide a sufficiently stimulating environment for the child?

For specific types of foster care, other qualities may be strongly desired. For example Ward (1987) lists some other specific qualities she would be looking for in an applicant(s) working with large sibling groups.

a) At least one parent must have a significant degree of admini-strative ability, to cope effectively with the diverse activities of a large family.

b) 'Unflappability' – to cope with all the unexpected incidents and crises in such a way that the family functioning is not too seriously disrupted.

c) The ability to promote healthy family interactions in family groups that may have developed unhelpful and negative relationships.

d) The ability to 'survive in the community', i.e., to be familiar with, and know how to find out about, community resources – recreational, educational and medical – and to know how to make use of them without producing excessive antagonisms.

It may appear a daunting list – and no doubt it could be extended further. The reality, of course, is that the prospective foster carers and their households with appropriate training and preparation, will have a range of those qualities and attributes, and will have them to a variety of degrees. They will vary over time depending on what else is happening in their lives. With continued support, post-approval training and experience they will continue to grow. In practice no foster family will have all the desired attributes all the time. The assessing social worker, and the Panel, have to be aware of, and accept, some weaknesses as well as strengths.

RELATING THE ASSESSMENT TASKS TO RESEARCH FINDINGS

A summary of key research findings have been provided in Chapter 1. Here, an attempt is made to relate some of these findings on foster carers to the assessment task.

Success is more likely when the foster carers are childless or have no children of their own of the same sex and age or younger than the foster child.

When the foster child's behaviour is felt to threaten the well-being of the foster carer's children, breakdown is more likely. From an assessment and selection point of view the key points here are that the foster carer's own children need to be secure and mature, and the household a tolerant one. Similarly, as pointed out in the previous chapter, the family's children have to be prepared and involved in the decision. However, the reality is, as Triseliotis (1989) puts it, 'If eventually there is no improvement most foster carers put the needs of their children first' (p. 13).

If foster carers do not perceive the child as having serious problems or, in the case of specialist foster carers, are able to respond to such problems, placements are more likely to succeed.

Foster carers do not usually mind being challenged, but by and large, they also like to feel that they are making some progress. They will frequently refer to uncertainty about handling problematic behaviour, a topic which they appreciate if properly handled on their training courses. Cautley and Aldridge (1974) devised a set of questions for prospective carers in which they had to respond to hypothetical situations dealing with problematic behaviour. Their research showed that the way in which prospective carers said they would handle such behaviour directly correlated to their success in practice, that is, people who answered the questions well, tended to go on and foster successfully.

It is a positive factor if the female foster carer is aged 40 or over at the time of placement.

Research findings on the age of the female foster carer are somewhat contradictory. Triseliotis (1989) reports that studies, mainly in long-term foster care, concluded 'that it is a positive factor if the female foster carer is aged 40 or over at the time of placement'. On the other hand, Adamson (1973) found that female foster carers who were under 40 combined a better understanding of the role with a better acceptance of the role in comparison to older carers. Dando and Minty (1987) offer support for this view. In view of the changing nature of foster care over the last twenty or so years and the variety of children now seen as fosterable, the age of the foster mother and foster father as predictors will have to be looked at more closely in relation to the type of fostering undertaken.

Where foster carers are inclusive of the family of origin there is also evidence of success.

Almost all the available studies are agreed about the importance of 'inclusive' fostering and the readiness of the foster carers to include the foster child's family in their plans and in their discussions with the child. The notion of inclusiveness also expects active encouragement to the parents to maintain contact with their child, eventually facilitating the child's return home. Among other things, the foster carer can also help complement the social workers' explanations to the child why he or she cannot yet live with their parents and what the plans are. The way issues of background information are shared and the child's family is perceived, can affect the child's self-image and sense of identity. The Children Act 1989, in a number of ways, strongly supports and reinforces the principles of 'inclusive' fostering. A willingness to work in this way must be an important aspect of assessment and selection.

When the foster carers are trained, prepared and supported following placement, sucess is more likely.

While in some respects these aspects reflect more on the agency than the carer, it is important in selection to note that carers who are trained, prepared and supported, are more likely to succeed. Cautley (1980), on the basis of her research findings, also places considerable importance on the inclusion of the male foster carer in the preparation process and all subsequent training.

If foster carers are experienced, successful placements are more likely.

While this is useful in planning placements it must be acknowledged that the Strathclyde Study Fostering and Adoption Disruption Research Project (1991) found that the most experienced female foster carers had the most disruptions, possibly because they were least supported, or had more difficult children placed with them. Dawson (1983) referring to long-term placements claimed that experienced foster carers were represented in over half the cases of maltreatment. McFadden (1984) made the observation that experienced 'good' foster homes were likely to be 'overloaded with high-risk children' enhancing the risk of children being abused in foster care. Cliffe and Berridge (1991) reported that breakdown in arrangements was often related to shortages of foster carers to enable matching between needs and skills, particularly for children displaying serious difficulties.

Factors in the Foster Carers' Family of Origin

Dando and Minty (1987), found from their study that if the foster carers had an 'unhappy childhood' they were more likely to be successful carers. They categorized more than half of those who said they had unhappy childhoods in the 'excellent' category and none were in the lowest category. It would be dangerous though to assume that negative childhood experiences *per se* equip people to care for other people's children. It needs also to be remembered that those featuring in this study were not a random sample of people with negative childhood experiences, but had been assessed and selected as suitable to act as foster carers. It can only be assumed that those whose negative experiences had left permanent scars were not selected and therefore did not feature in the study. Dando and Mindy's findings clash also with those of Tobis (1982) who found that female foster carers who abuse or neglect their foster children are more likely to have been abused as children themselves.

Male Prospective Foster Carers

Unlike most of the other research into foster care, Cautley and Aldridge (1974) who paid equal attention to male foster carers, identified a number of variables that seemed to contribute to greater placement stability. These include the male foster carer having a favourable attitude toward the social worker who is supervising the placement, toward the social worker's visits and suggestions about handling child behaviour, decision-making by couples, including those about money, along with a child-centred approach on the part of the male carer. Walsh (1981) too found that placement stability was enhanced when the male foster carer was emotionally involved with the child. Examples we came across include male foster carers taking children fishing, to football matches and attending school events. Overall, where a couple are joint foster carers, then the commitment and involvement of both to the care and management of the child are necessary for favourable outcomes.

Cautley and Aldridge (1974) also found that the way in which the female prospective foster carer talks about her own children is important. If she talks of each child as a distinct individual and mentions different characteristics for each one, this is a significantly favourable factor. The less she differentiates between her children, and the more she denies that anything about her children has caused her any concern or worry, the more favourable the outcome is likely to be, in terms of future fostering.

ASSESSMENT MODELS OR FRAMEWORK

As mentioned at the start of this chapter, Kirk's (1964) ideas of a group educative approach in the preparation of would-be adopters, was developed to take account of other ideas and requirements when selecting carers. As a result, ideas from the task-centred and systemic models, as well as from adult learning methods have been incorporated to form a new approach to assessment and selection. It is to the task-centred and systemic models that we now turn, but with a cautionary warning. Neither of these models provide a theory of human development. They are mostly frameworks helping us to organize material within certain principles. Knowledge for the understanding of human personality, motivation and aspects of behaving and relating still has to come from psychological theories of personality development, including psychodynamics. It is within this context that we set out to examine briefly the use of task-centred and systemic models in the assessment of foster carers.

The Task-Centred Model

Davis et al., (1984) set assessment firmly in a context of preparing prospective foster carers for the tasks that they will have to face when they are part of the fostering team. The whole of the approval process – preparation, assessment and training – is felt to set the tone for the future working relationship between foster carers and the agency. They particularly wish to avoid the 'dependency relationship', and the 'transference' referred to above. Their particular approach is through a combination of an assessment and training group linked to a home study undertaken by a 'link worker'. They see the aims of assessment as two-fold:

> We should come to know the family members well enough to ascertain their strengths and weaknesses, so that we will know

73

whether they can meet the tasks, whether they can work with us and what kind of resource they offer in terms of matching different children's needs . . .

and

. . . since the future working relationship between the foster family and the department should be open and honest, the process should have as little inequality of power in the relationship as possible. The sharing of information and of possible problems should be very open so that what we know, they know, and what they know, we know. The result should be agreement of what is possible and where any problems may lie, and mutual confidence in proceedings to the first foster placement. (Davies *et al.*, 1984, p. 16)

The assessment aspects of the group meetings are made explicit from the beginning. The group workers monitor the kind of personal contribution and group and marital interactions brought to the group and feed relevant information systematically to the 'link worker'. The link worker continues the role of course tutor to the applicants, gatherer of statutory and departmentally-required information and assessor. In their assessor role they use, apparently fairly eclectically, a variety of techniques – pen and paper excerises such as genograms, role-play, sculpting and the use of video. The observation of the interaction between family members and link workers (who often work in pairs) becomes 'at least as important and possibly more important' than the factual information that has been gathered.

There are of course strengths and weaknesses in this approach. Hunter (1989) found that applicants valued openness and sharing with agency workers, which is a strong commitment in the task-centred approach. Hunter also reports that 'where group work is taking place before selection, most families view (and seem largely to accept) it as part of the assessment whether project workers acknowledge it or not' (p. 36). Making the assessment aspects explicit prevents different perspectives developing between social workers and applicants, and helps establish honest working relationships. However, not all studies have found such a positive response to assessment groups. Rhodes (1992) reported that applicants felt themselves to be 'exposed to the public scrutiny of both social workers and other applicants' and that this insecurity was intensified by the knowledge that they were being formally assessed. 'Almost everyone,' she reports, 'felt inhibited by not knowing how other participants would react' (p. 207). These feelings were particularly strong among black applicants in a racially-mixed group.

This model lays a lot of emphasis on the social workers, both in the group and in the home study, observing the applicants interacting with each other, with other applicants, with their family and with agency workers. Though the evidence is still sketchy, nevertheless it suggests that group preparation/training contributes to greater satisfaction among carers and to increased placement stability (Triseliotis, 1988). On the other hand, Rhodes (1992) maintains that applicants in the groups still 'played the game of impression management' (p. 33). In her interviews, some applicants acknowledged that they had tailored their answers to what they thought the social workers wanted to hear, others admitted to withholding information or even lying 'for fear of offending other participants or of giving a bad impression to the Social Workers' (p. 33). That is to say that the applicants tried to respond to the exercises in ways which would fit with the model of good parenting that they thought the social workers were operating under. As the groups progressed and they picked up more clues and signals from the social workers, the applicants could adjust their self-presentation accordingly. The logic of Rhodes' comments is that those who would do best in this kind of assessment would be those who were most adept at playing this game.

Rhodes was mainly researching the experiences of black applicants and found that they were likely to be doubly disadvantaged in this 'game'. This is because the social worker's values and attitudes are very likely to be based on the white family structures and culture, and the black applicant may well find it harder to 'tune-in' to the finer messages to respond appropriately. White applicants on the other hand will have a head-start. Furthermore, black applicants, by being a minority in racially-mixed groups, felt constrained to play down cultural and ethnic differences because of a desire to 'belong' and the fear of antagonizing the white members of the group. If, as already outlined, 'traditional' individual assessments are pregnant with the possibility of subjectivity and misperception, can the multi-layered complexity of group interaction be any less so, unless groups are used solely as educative tools as suggested originally by Kirk in 1964?

The Cautley Questionnaire

Based on their research, Cautley and Aldridge (1974) developed a questionnaire which they maintain, when used in association with other information, can be a useful predictive assessment tool in the selection of foster carers. Apart from factual information and questions asked about couple relationships and relationships with children, some questions ask how the applicants would handle particular behaviours displayed by a child. The authors warn that their questionnaire is meant to be an aid to social workers to be more objective in their judgement and not a mechanism for replacing judgement.

Some aspects of the questionnaire, such as the emphasis on 'differentiation', would seem to link in with what might be called an 'ecological systems' perspective, and therefore it is perhaps not surprising to find the questionnaire used as an integral part of the assessment process in Anderson's 'A Systems Theory Model for Foster Home Studies', and referred to in McFadden's 'Preventing Abuse in Foster Care' (1984) which has a strong emphasis on practice derived from systems theory.

The Systemic Model

The systemic perspective is not so much concerned with individuals except in as far as they are part of a system or sub-system. It is particularly relevant when looking at the structure of the family, its flexibility, its interactions and how a child might be able, or be enabled, to fit in. The closeness or distancing of relationships, the quality of communication and feedback, as well as roles and rules undertaken or carried out by family members, can be examined within the systemic framework. The framework views the family as developing its own saga over generations which may have a powerful impact on current family members. Couple relationships can also be examined within the same framework.

A particular practice feature related to this approach is the use of diagrammatic assessment tools to help the worker and the family understand the system in which the family operates. The most familiar of these are the ecological map, or 'eco-map', the 'geno-gram', and 'structured mapping'. The primary source for the first two of these is the work of Hartman (1978). The eco-map shows, according to Hartman

> . . . in a dynamic way the ecological system, the boundaries of which encompass the person or family in the life space. Included in the map are the major systems that are part of the family's life and the nature of the family's relationship with the various systems. The eco-map portrays an overview of the family in their situation; it pictures the important nurturant or conflict-laden connections between the family and the world. It demon-strates the flow of resources, or lacks and deprivations . . . [it] highlights the nature of the interfaces, and points to conflicts to be mediated, bridges to be built and resources to be mobilised. (p. 471)

That is to say, it is not just a useful device for describing the system, but also for seeing what changes need to be made within the system to enable it to function more effectively.

Someone making an eco-map begins by drawing a diagrammatic representation of their nuclear family in a large circle in the centre of the map. This is done in the form of a family tree or genetic chart. When this is completed, the connections between the family and other parts of its ecological system are added. These are represented by circles outside the nuclear family's circle, each circle representing something such as 'work', 'extended family', 'school', 'friends' etc. The nature of the connection between these systems, and the family, are then either written in, along a connecting line, or represented by the type of line drawn (e.g., a dotted line would indicate a tenuous relationship). Some connections will link with the family as a whole, others to individual family members.

The main value of the eco-map is its visual impact, and its capacity not only to organize a great deal of factual information, but also the relationship between systems. Hartman claims, 'The connections, the themes and the quality of the family's life seem to jump off the page and this leads to a more holistic and integrative perception' (p. 467).

McFadden (1984) has adapted the eco-map specifically for one with foster families. She sees it not just as an assessment tool, but

as a constructive planning device prior to the making of placements. The worker and the family can add to the map the stresses
and resources which would be associated with placement.

While the eco-map places the family and individuals in their
ecological system, the genogram places them in the context of
time and what Hartman refers to as 'the family saga'. Anderson
(1982) gathers most of her information about applicants in the
form of a genogram, which she describes as 'a social and
emotional history'. The information includes

> dates of births, marriages, divorces, re-marriages and deaths of
> parents, spouses and siblings; jobs or educational histories; lines
> of closeness and distance; and information about changes in
> relationship to parents over the years. Also included are adjec-
> tives to describe members of each applicant's family as (the)
> applicant remembered them as a child. (p. 37).

She goes on to say that all this information gives the worker

> clues to the degree of losses experienced by the family them-
> selves of success or failure, possible projections . . . and capacity
> for growth and change. The genogram gives one a sense of the
> culture of the family applying to care for a child. (p. 41)

The third pen-and-paper device is the 'structural map'. This has
been adapted from Minuchin's work on family therapy (Minuchin,
1978) and looks more closely at the functioning and structure of the
nuclear family. In the mapping process, the roles family members
carry out, the lines of authority within the family, coalitions between
family members and boundaries between family subsystems are
drawn diagrammatically on paper. The map can highlight conflict, the nature of boundaries and the appropriateness of roles.

The social worker's task in the mapping process is to facilitate
the would-be foster family in assessing and describing their current
family structure. Having done that they can then begin to look at
how a potential foster child would fit in, and how positions within
the family might shift.

A strength of all these tools is that they bring the applicant's own
children much more clearly into the picture. Despite the fact that
placement disruptions are more likely when the well-being of the
foster carer's own children are threatened (Triseliotis, 1989), the
role of foster carer's own children is a very neglected area of study

and concern. The diagrammatic approaches can show visually the dynamic affects that a child moving into the family will have on children who are already there.

No assessment approach can entirely avoid manipulation and misrepresentation by applicants who have a strong desire to be approved. However, the systems approach, in conjunction with the Cautley Questionnaire, goes some way to making the assessment process more open and objective and less dependent on the intuitive judgement and flair of the individual worker.

EQUAL OPPORTUNITIES AND ASSESSMENT

It may be unrealistic to expect that complete objectively will prevail in all assessment work. Intuition remains a valued asset. The assessment process is an interactive human process whatever model is employed. Consequently inherent in the assessment process is the risk and fear of bias and prejudice.

By putting themselves forward for approval or non-approval, foster carer applicants place themselves in a subordinate position to the agency and its social work staff. This power imbalance may be reinforced by a wide range of factors in the wider social context. The social worker will be a 'professional' person, the applicant may well be a non-professional. The social worker may well be white, the applicant, black; the worker middle-class, the applicant working-class; the worker heterosexual, the applicant homosexual, and so on. The assessment process may well feel very different from either end of any or all of those spectrums.

Earlier in this chapter we referred to extra difficulties experienced by black applicants. In particular, Rhodes (1992) makes a powerful case that

the black applicants were doubly disadvantaged: not only were the social workers' standards likely to have been based on a 'white' profile of family life, but the white applicants were likely to have been more familiar with the 'rules of the game' and more proficient at playing it (p. 207).

Unfortunately, as Rhodes shows, cross-cultural assessments are not easy, and well-intended efforts to overcome these difficulties could often backfire.

While many black applicants were not happy with the process, neither were the white social workers, some of whom felt that they were not competent to carry out cross-cultural assessments. There is clearly a major need for training on non-oppressive practice for all social workers involved in assessment work, wherever they fit in any of the spectrums referred to above. There is also a need for appropriate advice and support to be at hand, so that workers can function positively in an aware and sensitive manner. The British Agencies for Adoption and Fostering (BAAF), in their Practice Note No 18, Recruiting Black Families (1991) lays emphasis on a number of points. It argues, in essence, for the importance of social workers approaching assessment in an open-minded way, looking at whether applicants will be able to meet a foster child's needs, not whether they will be able to meet them in a particular traditionally acceptable way, and looking at whether families function successfully, not whether they function in a way which might be expected from a Eurocentric perspective. The applicant's anxieties will be eased by greater honesty and openness in the assessment process. Applicants should be made fully aware of what the process is, and why the processes and procedures are necessary. Assessment issues should be clarified with the applicant, and assumptions tested.

The aim of assessment is to arrive at a conclusion with the applicants as to what they have to offer to foster care. This should be the case with all applicants, wherever they fit in the social and cultural spectrum. Furthermore, all applicants should be made aware of the venues that are open to them for appeals and complaints if they feel that they have not been treated fairly.

5 Foster Carers and Social Workers: the Working Relationship

INTRODUCTION

Foster care has never been a static entity providing the same kind of service to the same kind of children. We have already seen how foster care has developed. Today's foster carers have an interesting line of ancestors – the wet nurses, the industrialists and the ladies of the great houses whose interests were often served by the children themselves rather than the other way round. Although not static, foster care has always been grounded in childcare social work practice or, as Judy Stone puts it, 'History shows that foster care is developing all the time to meet the needs of different childcare policies' (1990, p. 56).

Nor has foster care been neutral. It has found itself associated both with permanent substitute care and again more recently with family support and supplementary care. As a consequence, the fortunes of fostering fall or rise and so too does the status of foster carers themselves. Not only are these fortunes closely related to what happens to residential care but it is also claimed that the attention paid to adoption for children with special needs and to specialist fostering has held back developments in foster care overall (Southon, 1986; Shaw & Hipgrave, 1989b).

It is suggested that in the 1980s carers who were approved to bridge children to adoption or to independence received far more in the way of social work and financial, group and training support than did their mainstream foster carer colleagues. (See, for example, Barnardo's 1981; Devon 1981; Shaw & Hipgrave 1983, 1989a & b; Westacott 1988; and Hazel 1990.) Yet, despite all the efforts, those specialist foster carers in receipt of a first-class support service numbered very few. In their extensive study of the beginning and ending of placements over two years in six local authorities, Jane Rowe and her colleagues say, 'The day-to-day bread and butter work of fostering is still the placement of younger children needing care for a brief period during a family crisis or to give relief to hard-pressed parents, (Rowe *et al.*, 1989, p. 79).

We know that a great many children looked after in public care are placed with non-specialist temporary foster carers. Berridge and Cleaver (1987) put the figure at 10,000 children each year in England and Wales and Triseliotis (1989) says that approximately two-fifths of children in care are placed with short-term foster carers, almost as many again with intermediate foster carers and the rest in long-term fosterings. In comparison the numbers of children fostered by the specialist carers are very few indeed (Lowe, 1990).

The recent move, referred to in an earlier chapter, towards treating all foster carers similarly should help to redress some of the imbalances outlined above. Already many local authorities are now transferring the lessons and the resources of specialist fostering schemes to their wider fostering workforce. For example, they are taking the lead in providing better standards of training, preparation and support from well-organized and resourced family placement units, fairer financial arrangements and greater opportunities for foster carer participation (see for example, Maclean, 1989 and Godward, 1991). When permanency is used to refer to the keeping or restoration of children to their families of origin, the role of foster carers is highlighted and strengthened. For example, the provision of short-term respite care in an attempt to prevent long-term family breakdown is of crucial importance.

This chapter mainly aims to address the relationship between foster carers and social workers as they together face the challenges of the initial post-Children Act years. More specifically, how can the social worker, as the fostering agency's personal and professional representative, assist and monitor the foster carer's practice? Which features of that working relationship are most helpful and productive? And how can the social worker best ensure that a working partnership with foster carers is formed and sustained in order to provide high standards of service to children and their families?

THE ROLE AND FUNCTIONS OF SOCIAL WORKERS IN RESPECT OF THE FOSTERING TASK

We have seen in the previous chapter that a number of descriptive prefixes have been attached to the foster carer's job title: professional, specialist, bridging, respite, remand and so on. Likewise distinctions are also drawn in respect of social workers whose tasks bring them into contact with foster carers. In practice, most local authority fostering agencies have established two types of social workers: one social worker for the child and one for the foster carers. So there are those who are responsible for children, their families and the individual care plans and there are those who perform specialist duties with regard to the recruitment, assessment, training support and review of foster carers. The first are generally referred to as the child or children's social workers. The second are variously called fostering officers, homefinders, or link or family placement social workers. The term 'homefinder' implies a greater emphasis on the recruitment rather than the retention of foster carers and the term 'fostering officer' carries connotations of a worker distanced from the mainstream of social work as though they were not social workers at all. Except for direct quotation I shall use the term 'link social worker'. It is a term commonly used to describe social workers engaged in family placement work. It also acknowledges an important aspect of their role of liaising between all the various parties. Volume Three of the Children Act 1989, Guidance and Regulations (Department of Health, 1991) acknowledges this social worker distinction.

> The role of the child's social worker includes support, advice and assistance to the foster parent, in relation to that child. It is desirable, however, for foster parents to be allocated their 'own' social worker to whom they may turn for general advice and support. (paragraph 3.58 p. 32)

Practice developments continue to emphasize the distinction between children's and link social workers. For example, social workers for children tend to take the lead in drawing up agreements in respect of each child's foster placement and the child's subsequent statutory reviews. Link social workers meanwhile tend to take the lead both in establishing a foster care agreement for newly approved carers and in attending to their regular performance reviews. Written agreements have become an important tool in the practice of all forms of social work. As already outlined in the previous chapter they are also particularly important in foster care especially when a child is accommodated and the formal and informal relationships between all the parties to a working partnership have to be supported by a carefully negotiated agreement. Agreements are also vital for new and inexperienced foster carers who will need more support from both types of social workers as they develop their fostering practice.

The distinctions are also recognized by foster carers themselves. In a recent study (Sellick, 1992) foster carers identified two main tasks for link social workers: they helped them to develop their foster care practice and they liaised with the children's social workers. On the other hand, carers looked to the child's social worker for more immediate practical and emotional support in relation to particular children for whom they were caring. This distinction is crucial for the next section which considers how foster carers view and evaluate the service delivery of both types of social workers. However, it is important to remember that unless referring specifically to the services provided by either link or children's social workers there are times when both provide similar and overlapping services to foster carers.

COMPONENTS OF AN EFFECTIVE WORKING RELATIONSHIP BETWEEN SOCIAL WORKERS AND FOSTER CARERS

Effective working relationships between social workers and foster carers begin with the carers feeling that they are valued both as people and as practitioners. They also respect social workers who acknowledge the price their children and partners have to pay. Foster families inevitably end up having to share more of their time, privacy, possessions and relationships.

One way of showing carers they are valued is when the social worker employs active methods of intervention. For example, a carer spoke with respect about a link social worker who liaised successfully on her behalf with the child's social worker. She described the link social worker:

> Always really on the ball. I'd have a word with her. She was straight in writing memos, speaking to her, trying to get things sorted out. Things like that which was a great help. It wasn't just me having to struggle. She was on our side, backing us up, making some of the running as well. (Sellick, 1992, p. 60)

These sorts of phrases – 'being on the ball', 'giving us backing' and 'making some of the running' – were used often by carers. Social workers demonstrated these when they actively listened to foster carers, showed an interest, developed a rapport and put aside time to talk. Foster carers have been identifying such positive qualities for some considerbale time. More than a decade ago, Endlestein (1981) listed 'caring, warmth, respect, empathy, hope and the desire to understand' (p. 468) as qualities which the North American foster carers in her study valued in social workers. Similarly, Hoggan (1991) in describing post-placement support services for new adopters in a Scottish local authority says that to be effective, they 'should be varied, flexible, available and ungrudgingly given' (p. 29). Other studies identified the need for praise and reassurance, rapport and energy (Littner, 1978; Cautley, 1980; Stone & Stone 1983, and Southon 1986).

It is often difficult to separate personal from professional qualities and indeed it seems that the two are interdependent. For example, there is no doubt that social workers need to be competent. Ineffective ones, no matter how personally skilled, will not contribute to the establishment of a working relationship if they do not familiarize themselves with departmental procedures to ensure that foster carers get paid their allowance or fees, are invited to training sessions and support groups, receive compensation for loss or damage, and are included as full participants at child care reviews and conferences. As one carer put it

> There were a lot of meetings that we did not know about until weeks or months afterwards and we were not a part of them. We were not a part of everything that happened to those youngsters while they were in our care. It caused quite a lot of upset with us. We felt undervalued. It created a lot of bad feelings which have gone on. They have left their mark (Sellick, 1992, p. 66).

This absence of participation is clearly not an experience unique to that foster carer. Another study which examined the experiences, perceptions and attitudes of short-term foster carers towards birth family contact in two local authorities (Waterhouse, 1992) concluded that foster carers did not feel in practice that they are given sufficient status, information, influence or authority to act as working partners with social workers.

This is a particularly alarming situation confirming as it does earlier studies in the US which charcterized agency practice as giving little direct participation in decision-making to foster carers and not consulting them about plans for children (Pasztor & Burgess, 1982). In Britain, a study of 300 statutory childcare reviews in one local authority found that many of them were held in social work offices rather than in the homes of foster carers. 50 per cent of which lasted only ten minutes or less (Sinclair, 1985).

Admittedly Waterhouse collected her data before the implementation of the Children Act. Yet about that time the Department of Health was issuing a handbook of guidance (Department of Health, 1989b) and later a consultative paper (Department of Health, 1990) both of which stressed the need to share information with foster carers and to involve them as full participants of the planning process. The Guidance and Regulations accompanying the Children Act (Department of Health, 1991) is unequivocal in requiring

- a written placement agreement with the foster carer covering a range of relevant matters in respect of the individual child placed, what is to be expected of the foster carer and the agency, and what has been agreed with the parents;
- a written statement of information for foster carers including the placement's objectives and the authority's plans;
- the child's personal history, state of health, educational needs, religious persuasion, cultural and linguistic background and racial origin are to be written down for the foster carers and
- where there is a special reason for withholding significant information, the reason should be recorded on the child's case record.

In short, 'the purpose of providing information is to enable the foster parent to care for the child' (paragraph 4.14, p. 35).

A foster carer spoke with feeling regarding a lack of information when he commented:

> I can understand you can't always give all the information at one time. Certain things: family circumstances, maybe legal things or medical requirements like HIV are done on a need-to-know basis. But surely a specific amount of information must be given to the foster carers instead of us having to ask all the questions. You shouldn't have to dig. (Sellick, 1992, p. 54).

The case for foster carer participation within a context of teamwork has been made elsewhere in a number of studies which highlight some of the ingredients of the fostering task. Most emphasize the 24-hour nature of fostering: even with excellent support from social workers including outside of office hours, foster carers remain front-line practitioners requiring full information to practice effectively and in the best interests of children. Foster carers need negotiating skills as they involve themselves in making written agreements or, for example, crucially when dealing with parents of accommodated children who may wish to remove them from the homes of carers late at night or when parents are intoxicated (Thoburn, 1991a). A foster carer in Sellick's study was able to deal with a grandparent calling late one night because she was able to tell a well-informed duty social worker.

Foster carers, especially those with some years' experience of fostering, see themselves as independent practitioners who sell their services. They are not employees of social services departments, are not accountable through a line management structure like social workers, and do not universally benefit from the same range of service conditions such as paid annual leave, sickness benefit or superannuation schemes. They value their independence, yet accountability, as we shall see later, cannot be sidestepped.

ACCOUNTABILITY AND RESPONSIBILITY

Much of this discussion has focused on the needs and rights of foster carers: how social workers need to value them, offer advocacy and liaison, work actively in forging a working relationship with them, provide all necessary information and ensure that they are full participants. However, the statutory guidance informs us that in each case a balance must be struck between offering carers support (thus building confidence) and holding them accountable for the child's well being, (Department of Health, 1989a).

As far back as the 1930s, the annual report of the Ministry of Health (1934–35) remarked on this issue that whilst fostering was the right response for many children, this system can be a real danger unless properly supervised (cited by Parker, 1990, p. 63).

The notion of a supervisory relationship between social worker and foster carer was explored in an early study (Kline & Overstreet, 1972), which concluded that

> As he is not the legal parent the foster parent remains responsible to the administrative agency that represents the legal parents or the state. Consequently the agency must exercise a supervisory function as one component in its arrangements with foster parents. (p. 217)

Social work supervision has been considered extensively since then. There are clear parallels between the application of supervision between line manager and social worker and social worker and foster carer. They share the same objectives of enhancing career or practice development and the delivery of effective services. They also share the same values arguing for a participatory and open style of supervision which empowers and enhances the confidence of the supervisee. Most refer to three components of supervision: the administrative or managerial function; the educative or development function; and the support or therapeutic function. (See for example, Payne & Scott, 1982; Kadushin, 1985, and Hawkins & Shottet, 1989).

Administrative tasks include preparing the practitioners to undertake their tasks; their induction; the allocation and delegation of work; monitoring, reviewing and evaluating that work; and communicating agency policy, procedures and structures. Recently, there was an inquiry following the conviction and life imprisonment of a foster carer for the indecent assault and manslaughter of a child aged nine months, and the grievous bodily harm and wilful ill-treatment of another child of sixteen months at placement. The inquiry's report defined supervision as aiming to ensure management accountability, management of time, monitoring of records, completion of administrative tasks, setting of priorities and checking of work done (Derbyshire, 1990, p. 83).

The same inquiry also examined the different responsibilities of link and children's social workers. It cautioned link social workers against assuming an overly optimistic and unquestioning attitude towards foster carers, particularly experienced ones. It warned that they should avoid the danger of over-identifying with foster carers.

Those of us who have been engaged in family placement social work should know just what the panel of inquiry meant and those managers who supervise link social workers should familiarize themselves with the harrowing details of this report.

In its response the fostering guidance accompanying the Act (Department of Health, 1991) emphasizes the need for social workers to monitor the practice of foster carers. Yet it seems to place a heavier burden upon the social workers of children in placement:

> The standard of care should be observed and the child's bedroom sometimes seen. Some visits should be unannounced in order to provide a balanced perspective of the quality of life in the foster home. A foster parent presenting a 'brave face' would not alert a social worker to their need for help and support in a particularly stressful time in the placement (Regulation 4.21a, p. 37).

Clearly we should not become over-alarmed. Foster carers rarely kill or injure children in their care. Workers and carers are however often faced with the bread-and-butter issues of foster care. A child's social worker or parent may be dissatisfied with the level of material standards or the question of hygiene in a foster home, while a link social worker may view these as marginal but acceptable, knowing that the foster carer provides consistently high standards of emotional care to children. People will, of course, have different standards. Everyone needs to consult one another at times such as these so that the right balance can be struck between monitoring standards and supporting foster carers. Fostering agreements and reviews of carers should assist if conducted in an open and flexible manner.

The educative function of supervision is assumed through the organization of training sessions. However, individual social workers do have a role to play with foster carers which goes beyond facilitating group activities. These include assisting carers to prepare a child to move back home or on to another carer, to develop special skills in fostering a sexually-abused child (see, for example, Nobbs & Jones, 1988) or to deal with a particular child's withdrawn or aggressive behaviour. All are examples of the potential of educative social work supervision. Similarly, social workers and foster carers should discuss not only the child's achievements but also behaviour that may give rise to concerns in order to seek together possible solutions. Outside assistance is often available (see, for example, the NFCA's training pack 'A Problem Shared', NFCA, 1990a) to support social workers and foster carers as they work together. There may of course be a gap between what the social worker has learned in training – such as theories of child development, anti-discriminatory practice, or relevant law – and the experience a foster carer has gained simply by being a carer over many years supplemented by the occasional short training course. However the transmitting of knowledge to a foster carer, no matter how experienced, is a social worker's responsibility. Two foster carers from different local authorities, each with more than ten years' experience of fostering children, described their perceptions of the social worker's role. The first one said:

> It is about acceptance of each other's roles and recognizing that there are major differences between what a social worker does and what a carer does. And they are equally as important as the other one.

The second showed an understanding of the social worker's responsibilities by commenting

> I might not agree with what the department are saying but if I can see why they are doing or saying it, I accept that and we agree to differ. There's no bad feeling because ultimately at the end of the day they are responsible and if anything happens to this kid it is their heads that will be on the block. (Sellick, 1992, p. 64)

Support, the third element of supervision, is also as relevant to foster carers performing their task as it is to social worker's undertaking theirs. Both of them practice at the sharp end of child care and need help at times with job-related stress, with assistance in managing tension, and with the requirements of job satisfaction if they are to avoid burn-out. Supportive supervision can be provided at two levels: from individual social workers and from the fostering agency itself. This second source of support will be dealt with at length in the next chapter which includes an examination of the arguments for supporting foster carers from an agency perspective. The discussion here will highlight some of the personal and professional qualities of support offered by link and children's social workers. In so doing a connection will be made later in this chapter with what we have learned from a number of wider child care studies. We can also learn from the consumers of social work services, carers and clients alike, about the value to them of various social work qualities and competencies. Again, the parallels they draw from their different vantage points are both interesting and instructive to the social work profession.

A study of the support of short-term foster carers in four local authorities and two independent fostering agencies in England (Sellick, 1992), and the published accounts of the services provided to adopters and foster carers who offer permanent care to children with special needs in a Scottish local authority (O'Hara, 1986 & 1991) show a striking similarity with regard to support. Sellick (1992) writes

> Workers and managers who make themselves available on both a regular and emergency basis especially outside of office hours; who consult and inform carers; who offer recognition to foster carers for their work and for the personal costs to their families by, for example, the provision of respite and specialist support; and who combine a working relationship with a personal touch are valued. (p. 91)

Compare that to O'Hara (1986) who lists an interest and commitment to the carer, availability, reliability, trustworthiness, warmth, an ability to listen and competence over official matters. We will look again at these accounts in respect of agency provision in the next chapter.

THE WIDER CHILD CARE SCENE

The gradual move towards practice by the rule book and demonstrating competencies that can be measured has made it unfashionable to refer to social casework principles, and to the intangibles of practice. What possible use can they be to a profession edging towards the twenty-first century and how can they be relevant to contemporary social work with all its responsibilities and statutory instructions? At the risk of appearing unfashionable and out of touch with these shifts let us refer briefly to Biestek (1961) and Hollis (1964). Biestek refers to the person's need to be treated as an individual, to communicate one's own feelings, to be accepted, not to be judged, to make one's own decisions, and to have one's own secrets kept confidential (p. 135).

Neither he nor Hollis duck the dilemma of self-determination. Biestek says that this is limited by the exercise of the agency and the law, with Hollis adding, 'It is important that the client's right to self determination exists until it is demonstrated that the exercise of this right would be highly detrimental to himself and others' (p. 5).

Moving on a decade, Carl Rogers too has something to say which we believe has an even greater resonance and relevance to today's social work practice. His core conditions of client-centred counselling (see, for example, Thorne, 1991) add congruence or genuineness, acceptance or warm regard, and empathy to the casework principles of respect, confidentiality, non-judging and, again, acceptance. There is considerable overlap with a recent publication on the Children Act where the author cites the following from the DHSS publication 'Social Work Decisions in Childcare' as prerequisite qualities for creating the conditions for a working relationship or partnership

> Honesty, naturalness, reliability, keeping clients informed, understanding their feelings and the stress of parenthood, offering combined practical and moral support. They will need actively to help vulnerable parents retain their role as responsible authority figures. They need to be actively involved with families. (Freeman, 1991, p. 64)

Time may pass, political conditions may change and the administrative and statutory burdens upon social services departments may seem unbearable, yet, at heart, the qualities which social workers employ and which their recipients respect (be they client or carer) remain remarkably constant. By way of further emphasis, two major child care studies have added to our knowledge about social work qualities and competences which are, we believe, transferable to the social worker/foster carer relationship. Firstly,

Fisher *et al.*'s (1986) study had a great impact upon child care practice especially with regard to the notion of parental responsibility and the working relations between parents and social workers. It describes the experiences of the two in respect of children in care and compares the different views expressed by the participants of the 350 cases studied. Social workers were praised by parents even where they were at odds over what they each considered to be the children's best interests when social workers were open and honest and 'put their cards on the table'; consistently showed concern by staying in close touch with parents; exhibited a desire to involve parents in the decisions and activities of care; took parents seriously, and acted purposefully and in a businesslike manner, for example, by using written agreements or by discussing various options with parents.

If we were to substitute 'foster carer' for 'parent' and relate the amended version with earlier parts of this chapter, we can see the similarities. Through the following example we can also compare the words of one mother in the Fisher study who commented about her social worker, 'He never went behind my back and did something without telling me, he'd ask and come and discuss it' (p. 112), with the words of a foster carer quoted by Sellick (1992)

> A good social worker is one where you don't have to check up what work you are doing. You're both going in the same direction; although you do obviously check back and communicate where you are at any given time, it's almost unnecessary because you know where you both are. (p. 63)

Farmer and Parker (1991) studied case files in four local authorities in England, covering over 300 children who were returned home while they were still subject to care orders. They used the phrase 'purposeful social work', meaning that social workers had to be clear about their responsibilities; they needed to be persistent, and they needed to be flexible. In a later report Farmer (1992) adds, 'It was this clarity of purpose plus the ability to use their authority, combined with steady reliable visiting that seemed to mark out the most effective social work input' (p. 13).

The same writers also found that cases in which there had been continuous social work involvement during the period when children on care orders were returned home were significantly more likely to be successful than those marked by periods where no social worker was allocated. Similarly, in their study of break-down in 530 short-term, intermediate, and long-term foster place-ments in three contrasting agencies, Berridge and Cleaver (1987) found that frequent visits by social workers were associated with fewer placement breakdowns. Two-fifths of the short-term foster carers in their study were visited at least fortnightly and in these the breakdowns were only at a rate of 10 per cent compared to nearly 25 per cent in the less frequently visited remainder.

CONCLUSION

This chapter has examined the working relationship of social workers and foster carers by making a number of links from the literature and from practice wisdom. In brief, social workers need to support foster carers both personally and professionally yet they also need to monitor standards of practice and safeguard the interests of children and families. The literature on the use of supervision in social work offers a good deal of practical advice which enables balances to be struck. The remarkable similarity between what carers and clients say they value from social workers stands out very clearly from the research. The combination of personal and professional qualities and competencies is high-lighted further by reviewing casework and counselling principles. Table 1 at the end of this chapter offers a visual summary of these. It also offers a picture of the social worker, foster carers and children and families linked in a circular relationship with one another, each having responsibility to the other, in other words, a partnership of care. It describes social workers as providers and foster carers and clients as recipients of services. There is of course a power imbalance but one which should not be characterized by a lack of participation on behalf of the recipients. It also has potential for development. In particular, foster carers are also providers, for example, those who offer respite care or who participate in frequent contact arrangements between children and families. They will provide a more sensitive and effective service if they are taught the lessons which social workers themselves have learned.

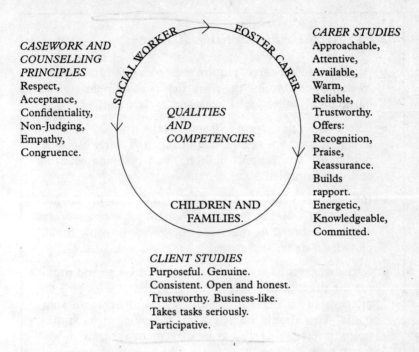

CASEWORK AND
COUNSELLING
PRINCIPLES
Respect,
Acceptance,
Confidentiality,
Non-Judging,
Empathy,
Congruence.

QUALITIES
AND
COMPETENCIES

CHILDREN AND
FAMILIES.

CARER STUDIES
Approachable,
Attentive,
Available,
Warm,
Reliable,
Trustworthy.
Offers:
Recognition,
Praise,
Reassurance.
Builds
rapport.
Energetic,
Knowledgeable,
Committed.

CLIENT STUDIES
Purposeful. Genuine.
Consistent. Open and honest.
Trustworthy. Business-like.
Takes tasks seriously.
Participative.

Table 5.1   Qualities valued by social workers, foster carers, children and families in relationships with one another.

KEY POINTS FOR PRACTICE

- Approved foster carers require their own link social worker to be responsible for their practice development and for liaising with other social work and agency staff.

- Effective support springs from social workers who apply energetic methods of intervention, such as active listening, persistence and rapport-building, and by being available and well-informed.

- Information which is clear and complete is the cornerstone of a working partnership between social workers and foster carers. As much information as possible should be written down and shared.

- Social workers have a responsibility to manage and monitor the practice of foster carers in order to safeguard the interests of children and families and to maintain standards. This should be achieved by regular visits and by training sessions as well as by placement agreements and foster carer reviews.

- Social workers are seen as helpful when perceived as knowledgeable, authoritative and purposeful, available, reliable, consultative, empathic and concerned.

6 Supporting Foster Carers: The Responsibilities of Fostering Agencies

INTRODUCTION

In the previous chapter, detailed consideration was given to the ways in which social workers as individual practitioners can support foster carers in carrying out their tasks and functions. Support from both link and children's social workers is one of the most important sources of support available to foster carers. Arguably it is the most important and is certainly the area most frequently cited by foster carers themselves. Well-informed, purposeful and competent social workers who work hard to establish a collaborative working relationship with carers can achieve much. In particular, they can help them to develop their foster care practice and to establish themselves as part of a team working together with others to deliver effective and high-quality services to children and their families.

Social workers who combine these skills with a number of personal qualities are even more effective in their work. Those who establish a trusting working relationship with carers and who value them by developing a rapport and by respecting the full contribution which foster carers make can help them through the most difficult and challenging parts of the job. This working relationship can sustain carers who, for example, are faced with the demands of aggressive or withdrawn children, frequent family contact arrangements, and complex departmental policies and procedures.

There are, however, a range of other methods which can provide additional and complementary sources of support to foster carers. Social workers are often instrumental in arranging these on behalf of the fostering agency which is normally the local authority social services department. But other staff both from within and beyond the agency are also of crucial importance in providing, facilitating and empowering foster carers to gain access to these other sources of support. From within the fostering agency these members of staff include social work managers, trainers, personnel and finance officers. Staff from other agencies include psychologists, doctors and teachers. One other group, foster carers themselves, are of vital importance in offering support to their fellow carers. Between them these people can provide the full range of support methods to carers – training, finance, respite care, support groups and local associations, specialist advice and mutual support. Each will be considered later in this chapter. First, it is important to consider why it is so necessary to provide support to both new and experienced foster carers.

THE CASE FOR SUPPORT

What are the arguments in favour of support? In essence there are three component parts. Supporting foster carers maximizes their retention, minimizes their costs to agencies and prevents the breakdown of the children's placements. In other words, support keeps carers, cuts costs and prevents placement breakdowns. At times, of course, these overlap. For example, poorly supported placements which break down may lead to foster carers giving up fostering altogether. Similarly, keeping foster carers and reducing their turnover lessens agency costs.

Retaining Foster Carers

A number of studies have identified the support from social work staff, finance, support groups and respite care as potential retainers of foster carers. New carers in particular require reassurance and encouragement from social workers and they need to feel valued by them. We know from one recent and extensive study of 2,964 foster homes in 13 English social services departments that 'hundreds of families are giving up fostering each year because they feel undervalued and unsupported' (Bebbington & Miles, 1990, p. 301). In one study, it was found that some foster carers who were dissatisfied with the level of support from local authorities joined an independent fostering agency instead (Sellick, 1992). These agencies have emerged in recent years because local authority foster carers and social work staff became independent in order to offer local authorities foster placements for those children whom they had found difficult to place with their own approved foster carers. They offer extensive support methods and the foster carers who work for these agencies report very favourably on them. Bebbington and Miles (1990) for instance comment

It is noteworthy that by comparison with local authorities these agencies appear to place emphasis on factors linked to foster family retention, such as substantial group support, respite care and high fostering payments. (p. 302)

Minimizing Costs

The long-held belief that fostering costs considerably less than the residential care of children has led to the expansion of the foster care service in the United Kingdom. The report of the Curtis Committee which preceded the Children Act 1948 used this argument to encourage the expansion of fostering after the Second World War. Indeed the argument can be traced as far back as the Poor Law whereby children who were 'boarded out' with families cost the Poor Law guardians considerably less than accommodating them in the institutions of the time.

Figures were published by the Department of Health in the mid-1980s which estimated that foster placements cost an average of £42 per child per week compared with £304 for a child in residential accommodation (Knapp & Fenyo, 1989). It is now clear however that the payment of expenses and allowances to foster carers make up only a small proportion of their overall costs though even these are increasing. The recruitment, training and assessment developments of the foster care service contain hidden costs associated with social work and administrative staff time. Additionally, services which foster children receive such as psychological counselling and speech therapy add considerably to the costs involved. To put it simply, fostering is no longer a cheap option. The investment of public funds in recruiting foster carers will be wasted if they are not retained by the provision of a range of support methods. Furthermore, the argument for foster care must be made on its merits and not on its costs.

There is another argument. Evidence is emerging that those local authorities which pay their carers a fair income and who provide the range of other support methods, especially good social work support, attract new carers and retain their existing ones. These local authorities tend to be found in our large cities and conurbations. Their gains are often at the expense of the rural and suburban local authorities which border them. National and local newspapers have reported this phenomenon and were starkly portrayed by one study (Price, 1992) which found that 'the discrepancies are such that Strathclyde pays higher allowances for a four year old than Dyfed pays for a teenager'.

One county council increased allowances by 20 per cent to make it more competitive in recruiting and retaining its foster carers. In another the director of social services told his committee that a number of foster carers had moved to a more generous neighbouring authority which paid higher rates (Deane, 1991).

Preventing Placement Breakdown

The relationship between good social work support of foster carers and successful placement outcomes has been identified by many studies. The components of this working relationship include the easy availability of social workers, the amount of energy they expend and their attempts to build a rapport with foster carers.

THE METHODS OF SUPPORT: A SUMMARY

Having then argued the case in favour of supporting foster carers, let us turn to an examination of support itself. British and North American literature had addressed itself to this topic over the past 15 years or so. Research studies and the published accounts of social work practice with people who both foster and adopt children in public care have grown during this period. This is as a result, in part at least, of increased recruitment efforts by social work agencies who wish to keep the carers they have recruited and by the phenomenon of foster and adoptive placement breakdowns.

An important element of this literature has been the expression of the carers' own views. In other words, carers as consumers of a support service have had their experiences examined and their views expressed in this literature.

Perhaps the most striking feature to emerge is the similarity of views of both short-term foster carers and the parents who have adopted special-needs children with regard to support. Despite the different roles and tasks of temporary fostering and adoption, the issues which matter to those who undertake them are remarkably alike. Two sources referred to in the previous chapter highlight the main sources of support which matter to carers.

First, O'Hara (1991) recommends the following list of support services in order to meet the needs of adopters. (The same agency (Lothian) is extending similar services to all its foster carers).

- Every family should be supported by their social worker and the child's social worker at least up to the time of granting the adoption order and beyond as needed.
- The families' social worker should be available to offer a crisis intervention service after adoption if the adoptive family requires this.
- There should be a range of support and training groups after adoption available to families run in cooperation with the adopters themselves.
- Specialized psychological and psychiatric services with a real understanding of the dynamics of adoption of children with special needs should be readily available to families.
- The development, in partnership with adopters, of a peer group support network which can, with support from the adoption agency but independently, offer a range of services to families. For example:
  - General support meetings run by adopters;
  - Counselling services for adopters by adopters with specialist skills;
  - A 'listening ear' service when families are stressed and do not feel able to approach the adoption agency;
  - Babysitting service and befriending services which can give adoptive families the kind of support more usually available from the extended family or friends;
  - Finance, easily and regularly available, is vital to

> sustain these placements: approved adoption allowance schemes should be open to any family who request such assistance. Alternatively periodic payments to cover extra special needs can make all the difference to placements.

Second, Sellick (1992) summarizes the views of a sample of foster carers who provide short-term placements for children. They identify a remarkably similar list of services to support their work. These were:

- Reliable, accessible and personally skilled specialist social workers who liaise with other staff as well as helping them directly with the practical and emotional aspects of fostering.
- Children's and family social workers who provide immediate placement-related support including out-of-office hours.
- Relevant practice-based training with other foster carers and social workers.
- Support groups and informal networks of foster carers which enable them to share experiences and tackle common problems together.
- Adequate and sensitive respite facilities.
- Expert and accessible specialist advice especially from the health, psychological and education services.
- A reliable, realistic and fair income as well as efficient systems of financial compensation for damage to themselves and their homes and possessions.

A working group of London-based foster carers and social workers (the London Child Care Forum, 1988) identified the following areas of support:

- support which is responsive to the needs of black and ethnic minority carers;
- alternative points of contact in the absence of the link or child's own social worker;
- publicized arrangements for handling complaints and appeals, and
- clear arrangements for dealing with allegations against foster carers both in ensuring the provision of legal cover and in providing support for the family which is acceptable to them.

A FRAMEWORK FOR SUPPORTING FOSTER CARERS

The means by which fostering agencies provide support to foster carers will vary according to the type of support on offer and the level of participation of foster carers themselves. Some forms of support remain the sole responsibility of the agency, for example, the provision of social workers and financial support. It is the agency after all which employs and supervises social workers and which pays the allowances or fees to their approved foster carers. Other methods of support require the active participation of foster carers if they are to be as effective and successful as possible. Foster carers themselves are often actively involved in giving as well as receiving respite support to their fellow carers and are the main players in support groups. In these examples, fostering agencies should help set up or facilitate the support but foster carers should play a role in sustaining them for themselves. Other support methods, notably local foster care associations and less formal mutual support networks of carers, are usually established and led by carers with social workers playing only a minor role.

The table on the following page summarizes rather more visually the manner in which support can be offered and delivered to foster carers and places this service within a context of agency and carer partnership. It will be used to order the rest of this chapter and each support method (except for staff support, dealt with extensively in the last chapter and the beginning of this one) will be considered in turn.

Financial Support

Payment levels for foster carers vary widely across the country. Recent figures from the National Foster Care Association (NFCA) show that almost two-thirds of local authorities still pay allowances which are below the Association's recommended rates (Lowe, 1990). It is perhaps easy to understand why many foster carers would say that the inadequate fostering allowances they receive are no support at all.

The means of paying foster carers also varies. The minimum basic allowance is the commonest method of payment and is

Table 6.1 *Support through partnership*

Agencies . . . . Foster carers

Provide: Staff support
         Finance
         Training

                   Facilitate: Specialist advice
                   Respite
                   Support Groups

                             Empower: Local Associations
                             Mutual Support

(from Sellick, 1992, p. 102)

calculated to cover the cost of keeping a child. It includes therefore the cost of clothing, food, heating and so on. It is a sum which is not taxable, which does not require the foster carers to make National Insurance contributions and which does not affect their eligibility to state benefits such as Income Support or Housing Benefit. A single person with no children of their own aged under 16 years and caring for a foster child does not need to be available for employment and can therefore continue to claim Income Support and other benefits (Verity, 1988).

The basic allowance is sometimes enhanced to take account of a child's special needs which are particularly expensive. Special diets, frequent journeys to hospital and extra clothing can be paid for by enhanced allowances. In an attempt to match needs with cost and to avoid an expensive system of applying for each separate 'extra', some agencies have composited these extra costs and introduced a banding system often based on the discretionary judgements of its staff about the difficulties of the child. Although discretionary banding schemes attempt to meet the additional costs of individual children, they have a built-in financial disincentive. When a child's expensive behaviour lessens, so too does the amount of payment. For foster carers, says Southon (1986) in her study of overseas agencies, 'There is a natural desire to demonstrate what they have achieved but equally a reluctance to thereby throw away a higher rate of payment' (p. 86).

A system analogous to this is perhaps one which would reduce a teacher's salary once her pupils had learnt to read. Enhanced allowances which include a fee or reward for service element are taxable.

Payment of a taxable fee or element of reward has been a feature of specialist schemes for carers of teenagers (Lowe, 1990) or children who have special needs (Westacott, 1988). Some local authorities have extended these payments to short-term foster carers (Maclean, 1989). Foster carers who are paid fees are self-employed and, according to income levels, are liable to pay both income tax and National Insurance contributions. They also risk losing state benefits. As a result some agencies exercise creative accounting methods. One, for example, pays foster carers who are also benefit claimants enhanced allowances rather than fees. Likewise, one independent agency pays a low fee and correspondingly high allowance as a matter of course. Another local authority recommends payment of fees be made to a woman if her male partner already pays tax on a separate occupation in order to minimize their tax liability.

As both Sellick (1992) and Rhodes (1993) discovered, it is not only the level of rates but the process of payment which can be a source of discontent to foster carers. Rhodes, for example, comments, 'Foster carers complain that they have to ask for their entitlements, that they are made to appear "money grabbing" and that authorities are slow in making payments' (1993, p. 10).

Sellick (1992) discovered several instances across the country where foster carers waited months to be recompensed by local authorities for damage to their property while fostering. One foster carer, for example, told him that she had to wait 18 months to get paid the several hundreds of pounds it cost to repair structural damage to her house caused by a foster child. One local foster care association calculated that carers subsidized the local authority by as much as 50 per cent of inadequate payment levels. Overall, foster carers often describe how their goodwill and commitment are exploited by fostering agencies who pay too little and too late.

Many local authorities pay a very low proportion of the fostering allowance in order to retain a fostering placement and many have still not provided carers with insurance and indemnity schemes to compensate them for damage or for legal defence costs in the event of a complaint or allegation against them even though they have been under a duty to do so since 1988.

Yet when payment schemes work efficiently and fairly, fostering agencies benefit because their foster carers feel valued and supported. As Sellick (1992) puts it, 'Adequate payments efficiently paid, realistic rates for retainers and swift compensation for damage seem to lead to job satisfaction and respect for the agency and its staff' (p. 90).

PAYMENT: THE WAY FORWARD

The system of remunerating foster carers has not caught up with their tasks. Apart from the legacy that caring should be carried out for nothing, payment systems seem to stem from a definition of ensuring value for money based on keeping actual costs as low as possible rather than as a means of maximizing the welfare of children needing foster care services. A payment system should offer a choice of remuneration to all foster carers and end the divisive manner in which some specialist carers are paid differently and more generously than the remaining majority of foster carers. This does not mean payment of salaries to all carers. Indeed very few carers seem to wish to be paid a salary as they or their partners are already salaried in other jobs, or they know that they are likely to fare better on Income Support and other benefits than they would on a low fostering salary. Others feel neither motivated nor rewarded by the money nor do they wish to be. Their returns come instead from the children, their fellow carers, and from the fostering task itself. Some recognize the danger that, as salaried employees, their independence would be compromised and their low status would plummet further in a large organization like a social services department. Others fear that paid employment would stigmatize them in the eyes of parents who would see them as just another type of social worker.

However, a few carers would, if given the choice, take a salary. Some would choose to carry on receiving an allowance but one which would adequately cover the costs of caring for children; others would choose an allowance and a fee. Many foster carers take on additional tasks through supporting other carers and, sometimes, parents, belonging to agency panels and trusts, providing training and coordinating or leading support groups. In order to do so they should be paid a reliable and competitive income which would reward them for their time and skills.

Honorariums or sessional fees are clearly options in these circumstances. No method of payment is intrinsically better than any other and the risk of creating a divisive hierarchy of payments should be avoided. The mutual benefits of greater flexibility in paying foster carers are likely to be significant. For agencies, fairer and more efficient payments would allow them to review what they previously saw as social work tasks and transfer some of these to willing carers. They would also retain their trained and experienced carers and attract new recruits. For the carers, the ability to exercise choice over how they are paid would add recognition to their tasks and greater opportunities for career development within their agencies.

TRAINING

The content of foster carer training, especially in relation to selecting and preparing foster carers in a group setting, is dealt with extensively elsewhere in this book. Training programmes which introduce potential foster carers to the realities and challenges of fostering are provided by most fostering agencies and many use or adapt the NFCA's 'Challenge of Foster Care' training pack (NFCA, 1988). Such training is of great value to foster carers at the start or in the early stages of their fostering career. Few agencies, however, have developed ongoing training schemes for carers which are informed by the foster carers' own expressed training needs. Some carers feel that training is something which is imposed upon them to suit the needs and cost constraints of the agency. The impact upon Social Services departments of child sexual abuse, HIV infection and AIDS, and the needs of black children in care is reflected in the number of training programmes which specifically address these issues. All are valuable but, if training is to be truly supportive, carers need to be full participants in the choice, planning and, at times, running of training courses. Attention by agencies to the process as much as the content of training is vital. The single most important feature of training to many foster carers is that they should be trained alongside social workers. Agencies who have adopted this position have discovered that it is not only cost-effective but offers a very practical opportunity for workers and carers to work together as colleagues or partners.

This process carries with it other benefits. Once social workers and foster carers start training together, they begin to get to know one another away from the sound and fury of their day-to-day working lives. They begin to appreciate each other's needs and abilities and they begin to enjoy each other's company. Foster carers also seem better able then to work out what they would like from training. For example, tackling the complexities of family contact, learning how to negotiate a placement agreement, or how to contribute purposefully to a case conference or review can be fruitful developments which spring from the process of social workers and foster carers working together in a training session. Role-playing a sensitive contact visit when a social worker plays a carer, and a carer a parent, or some formal input from research about the benefits to children of contact, can be the stuff of effective and supportive training. There are of course resource implications and some agencies who expect foster carers to attend regular training pay them an attendance allowance or fee. Others pay travelling and child-minding expenses which foster carers incur. A few agencies have appointed 'teen-sitters' or other approved adults to cover for foster carers while they attend training sessions or planning meetings. Proper foster carer participation in training costs money but it can also deliver valuable returns to agencies. Training which offers recognition and support to carers and which makes them feel valued and equipped for their tasks is likely to create a satisfied fostering workforce who will not be minded to look elsewhere to foster.

SPECIALIST ADVICE

Many agencies have acknowledged for some time that adopters and long-term foster carers require additional sources of professional support to that provided by link and children's social workers. A number of child and family psychiatry departments offer consultation to carers who experience difficulties often from a family therapy perspective. (See for example Lindsey, 1985: Argent, 1988; Elton, 1988, and Rushton *et al.*, 1989.) Likewise the carers of children considered to have special needs or to be particularly hard to place outside of residential care settings have benefited from arrangements which offer them advice and counselling from specialist workers. The independent fostering agencies and some local authorities have facilitated this form of support.

One local authority has established a scheme to provide educational support to children in its care including the 56 per cent placed with foster carers (Briand, 1991). Foster carers here can get direct advice from education staff. Another local authority provides a comprehensive psychological service to everyone in its area involved in family placement including, of course, foster carers (Nissim, 1993). Most often the team of psychologists was involved in advising foster carers in respect of the range of disturbed behaviour presented by children and young people in foster placements. They also assisted foster carers in dealing with issues of family contact and education matters affecting children in their care. Foster carers are now entitled under the Children Act 1989 to participate in family centre activities and to seek appropriate advice, guidance or counselling.

Foster carers themselves have described the need for such specialist professional help in relation to particular children in their care. In the following two examples, the first carer describes the effect upon her of one particular child and the second, the emotional impact when a teenage girl disclosed to her that she had been sexually abused. Both do so at some length and with considerable feeling and describe how the whole foster family can be affected.

I was getting into such a state that I couldn't sleep at night. I was getting terrible pain in my neck and shoulder from tension. I was getting very irritable. You need someone to help you, someone professional to help carers with difficult children. Yes, the other carers are there but professionally you need proper help. And not just for you but for the whole family at times.

The second carer commented:

We had a disclosure. It was our first. I got pretty screwed up about it afterwards. Everybody was so upset about it because we just couldn't hold on to her. It just upset the whole family. It was very painful. I felt such a physical pain. I had to get my feelings out. I began to doubt what I believed in. I had to come to terms with my own feelings, to detach myself from it. I never expected to have the emotions I felt. (Sellick, 1992, p. 84)

The Fostering Guidance and Regulations (Department of Health, 1991) recognize the need for specialist support to foster carers: 'Foster parents should also have access to the support of professionals in other services which is available to all parents in the community' (paragraphs 5.5.9, p. 32).

As a response, agency staff have already begun to facilitate this support through discussions with local child psychiatric and psychological clinic staff and with staff from education departments. In their negotiations with these agencies, local authorities should clearly explain the role and task of fostering especially with regard to contact and would do well to directly involve representatives of foster carers in their discussions.

RESPITE CARE

The vast majority of adults who care for children benefit from opportunities which give them a break from their daily responsibilities. Parents can turn to their relatives or to babysitters, and youth workers, teachers and residential care staff go off-duty or hand over their responsibilities to their colleagues. Increasingly, foster carers are acknowledging this need for themselves. One, for example, said, 'It's important for us all to have a break to recharge our batteries – a breathing space so that we can get some strength back' (Sellick, 1992, p. 81).

Respite care can be a very effective way of supporting all foster placements but especially those which are under particular stress or threat of breakdown. The independent fostering agencies referred to earlier have taken the lead. Most encourage their carers to devise pairing arrangements which allow carers to 'caretake' other carers' foster children at regular intervals or at times of stress. Although informal, these arrangements presuppose that carers have been fully vetted and approved and understand through their own experience the needs and demands of foster children. They also seem to function without too much bureaucratic hindrance so that foster carers pay their fellow carers for the short periods when respite care has occurred.

Local authority fostering agencies are increasingly providing respite care facilities to their foster carers. Some expect carers to arrange respite amongst themselves and others provide additional resources such as specially approved sitters or residential and family centre facilities. Placement agreements have great potential here both to include planned periods of respite and to build in contingency arrangements at times of crisis. For children with special needs for example, shared care arrangements with a residential home can allow the foster carers to take evenings or weekends off or to have a holiday away. Day-care provision for younger foster children can operate much as it does for working parents.

Agencies should take the lead, consult with carers and determine together the best ways of facilitating respite.

MUTUAL SUPPORT

The support of foster carers by foster carers is a very potent form of support. Carers themselves report that there is nothing quite like it amongst the range of support methods for keeping them going and of preventing placements breakdowns. By meeting together in support groups, in training sessions and in informal and social gatherings, foster carers pass on practice wisdom, arrange respite, share experiences, tackle problems or simply avail themselves of the opportunity to offload safely.

Mutual support springs from a number of different sources. At times it is agency-led and at others it comes from the foster carers themselves. Most agencies form support groups. For example, in a study of the majority of local authorities and voluntary organizations in England and Wales which provide teenage fostering schemes, Lowe (1990) found that most of them provide monthly support groups usually led by link social workers. When groups for approved foster carers follow on from initial preparatory training groups, the support they offer sustains and consolidates earlier gains. It is important to distinguish between two main objectives of support groups: the self-help function when foster carers can share their practice experiences, and the training objective. It is not, of course, always possible or desirable to separate the two but it is crucial that foster carers have a real say in how their support groups function in order to sustain the life and vitality of the group. As Brown (1988) puts it

> There are few people that foster carers can truly talk to about rejection, stealing, lying or other problems without appearing to be failing in their role. With increasing confidence they are able to do so in the support group. (p. 165)

Support groups have great potential for empowering foster carers so that they are better equipped to work alongside social workers and other professionals in providing services to children and their families. In support groups 'traditional models of authority are replaced by roles which implicitly convey acceptance, respect and joint working' (Hutton, 1988, p. 175). As such, support groups of foster carers can challenge local authority practice and some have given carers the confidence to seek better conditions and payment or to have a greater say in planning training sessions.

The Fostering Guidance and Regulations (Department of Health, 1991) affirm the importance of mutual support in suggesting that social worker support for foster carers 'may be supplemented by links with an experienced foster parent' (p. 32). Some local authorities have acted upon this. One, for example, has established a formal method of recruiting, training and paying experienced foster carers to support their fellow foster carers with less than one year's experience or those with a particularly challenging placement (Cambridgeshire, 1990). These support foster carers meet formally and individually with carers, lead support groups and act as trainers. They are also easily accessible to their peers over the telephone at times when social workers may be unavailable.

Other local authorities encourage mutual support by subsidizing telephone helplines to foster carers. One local foster care association (see Bayliss, 1993), for example, provides a 24-hour telephone service offering advice, help and support to its foster carers which the local authority officially recognizes and publicizes to all new foster carers. These types of mutual support are considerably more effective than the out-of-hours duty system operated by local authorities. Duty social workers are usually too distant to offer any immediate help and because they cover all emergencies in an often large district are generally poorly informed about particular children and their carers. In contrast, fellow foster carers are generally available, informed and sympathetic and can refer on to the emergency social work service when necessary.

Local foster care associations which are generally affiliated to the NFCA, offer a more formal method of mutual support to foster carers. Through them representations can be made to local authorities over a wide range of fostering issues: payment, insurance, training and practice issues. Most fostering agencies have welcomed these and social workers attend the association meetings and social events. Some agencies encourage their carers to join by paying their annual subscription to the association or by making annual grants. Some Social Services committees have co-opted the chair or other officer of the association. All these are positive efforts by fostering agencies which show recognition to foster carers and empower them as full members of a foster care service.

CONCLUSION

Arguably there has never been a time before now when foster carers so needed the full range of high-quality support from fostering agencies. The continuing growth in the use of foster care placements for children of all ages, races and disabilities coupled with the demands of the Children Act 1989 and its Fostering Regulations and Guidance, have placed heavy burdens upon foster carers and their own families. Those burdens are only likely to be manageable through the provision of support so that placements can be maintained, foster carers retained, and agency costs contained. In particular, support can ensure that foster carers become fully integrated members of staff teams which provide services to children and families. Additionally the greater emphasis on contact between foster children and their families is being felt by foster carers at the sharp end of child care practice. Permanent foster carers and adopters as well as temporary foster carers are finding that some form of family contact is becoming the norm rather than the exception for children who they are looking after in the short term or raising into adulthood. The support provided to these carers by social workers is of paramount importance. Social workers themselves carry the burden of establishing and sustaining effective working relations with foster carers which stem from their own professional competencies and personal qualities. They are also pivotal in ensuring that other methods of support are effectively delivered to foster carers. They play a central role in the provision of relevant practice-based training and support groups, efficient and reliable financial support, adequate and sensitive respite arrangements, and expert and accessible specialist support. They can also encourage foster carers themselves to benefit from the enormous potential of formal and informal mutual support networks.

KEY POINTS FOR PRACTICE

- In addition to giving direct support to foster carers them-selves, social workers are instrumental in providing and facilitating a package of support services to carers, such as training, finance, respite care, support groups and local associations, specialist advice and mutual support.

- It is crucially important that fostering agencies support carers in order to maximize their retention, minimize the costs associated with high turnover of approved and trained carers and prevent the placements of children from breaking down.

- Research studies and the published accounts of carers as consumers of support services, refer to remarkably similar sources of support for both permanent and temporary carers alike.

- Fostering agencies which invest in the full range of support services gain a return on that investment in the form of valued, committed and loyal foster carers.

- The support which foster carers give to and receive from one another is of enormous importance. Maximizing these opportunities is eventually beneficial to the children.

7 Working with Children in Foster Care

This chapter outlines the main tasks involved when moving children to foster care, while they are in foster care and before moving them either back to their families, to adoption or to independence. Chapter 8 concentrates on the kind of facilitating techniques that can be deployed, including practical exercises, for encouraging and stimulating communication with children and young people in foster care.

It is recognized that the word 'children' covers a long age spectrum and that no single approach therefore can respond to the diverse needs of a group stretching in age from 0–17. No doubt age is not the sole criterion in choosing strategies for intervention with children, but it is an important one. The common concept which links the different periods in children's lives is that of communication. Useful ways of communicating with children can be based on individual or group work and sometimes on a combination of both, depending again on age and level of understanding. While the individual approach may be more appropriate when preparing children to move from their families, a combination of individual and group methods appear to suit particularly those children who are already in foster care or being prepared to move out of foster care.

THE EXPERIENCE OF SEPARATION

As others have pointed out, children who are about to be moved or who are in the care of social work agencies, can be 'anxious, uncertain and confused' about what is happening to them. They have often experienced disruptions and changes in their lives along with the loss of familiar people. Separation from familiar people has a personal and distressing impact on them. Younger children, though unable to put their experiences and feelings into words, are not affected any less. Neither does finding a child a 'nice and kind' residential, foster or adoptive home, automatically resolve some of the fears and anxieties. A child's world can still be populated with apprehensions. To a child, what happened before can also happen again. Each child, of course, experiences their situation differently, but separation anxiety, sadness, guilt, fear or mistrust can impair their capacity to relate or attach to the foster family. Even children who feel relieved when moved from abusive environments are not affected any less by the experience of separation (See Jewett, 1984.)

Direct work with children either before or after they move to foster care involves the social worker in becoming familiar with the children and their world, learning about their interests and abilities as well as about their fears and problems. It also requires meeting and talking to the people who are or have been important to them, ranging from parents and siblings to other carers. Eventually a relationship of trust has to be built up, which will allow for both reparatory as well as preparatory work to be done, in time for the move to the foster carers or to any new family. Because the social worker can become such a central figure in a child's life, with powers to remove and move, children may come to see social workers as very powerful people.

For many children, the social worker may also be the only link between them, their past and current life and the wider world. Even with older children, frequent changes of social workers, like frequent changes of carers, increase the child's isolation and mistrust of the adult world. Children in care usually refer with scorn to the successive changes of social workers before they even get the chance to know them. They are equally scathing towards those who fail to keep their promises. Planning for children and preparing them to move presupposes continuity in relationships and the capacity to communicate with them. Readiness to listen and willingness to understand are part of the communication skills required. While some of the children will be known to the worker well before they come into the care of the agency, for others there may have been no time to get to know them individually beforehand. As a result, some of the explanations may have to be done retrospectively.

Many children do not understand why they cannot live with their own parents, or are uncertain about themselves and where they belong. Not surprisingly, low self-esteem is often a characteristic of many children in care and foster care. Children who have to move away from familiar figures live in an unpredictable world with an uncertain future. As noted in another chapter, children are usually aware of this and it increases their sense of insecurity. They may also feel rejected and different from other children, harbouring sometimes a host of feelings and thoughts about their parents ranging from anger, to guilt, to idealization. Experience also suggests that even with explanations, children are often unclear and vague about their exact situation. These observations reinforce the view that explaining has to be part of a continued process, rather than a once-and-for-all explanation. Neither can assumptions be made about what they already know.

Corrigan and Floud (1990) also describe vividly what grieving children go through because of the loss of their attachment figure, even if it is a temporary one, and how under these circumstances their self-image becomes fragmented. They go on to suggest basic identity work to help children get in touch with their 'senses' and to reveal their feelings and thoughts. This process can then help them to deal with the first stages of their grief, that is, shock, rejection, anger and/or depression.

COMMUNICATING WITH CHILDREN

Verbal and non-verbal forms of communication are essential as means for helping children cope with the kind of feelings described earlier and for involving them in the process of planning. Communication can also have its own intrinsic value. Others too have pointed out that communicating with children and reaching them at an emotional level is notoriously difficult. Unlike with adults, formal interviews and exchanges do not usually work either with younger or older children. What usually happens is that most children withdraw or fail to respond. It is just not easy for children to tell an adult how they feel, and it can often feel too dangerous to reveal feelings. This does not mean that children cannot use words to share feelings or express views.

Whilst some children may be ready to relate early on, others require time and the opportunity to know and trust before they can do so. Ryan and Walker (1985) in their book describe a number of ways for helping children to talk about feelings. Most children before they reveal themselves will want to see and experience the worker as a real person and to assess the worker's attitudes and intentions towards themselves (see Winnicott, 1984). Until then, communication may be stilted. (For more detail see the BAAF pack on Communicating with Children, 1991.)

Because a direct approach to communicating with children is not often easy, one useful indirect technique suggested by Winnicott (1984) is what she calls the value of the 'third object'. 'In the majority of cases', she adds, 'it helps to have something between us and the child, a third thing going on which at any moment can become a focal point to relieve tension' (p. 84). In this connection car rides can be important, or it may be drawing, or swimming, playing or walking round the garden, or even the presence of the cat or dog or whatever. For example, there are many interesting games that can be played without the use of words, even throwing a ball, which can be very useful in helping to establish an initial contact with non-verbal or very young children. Depending on the child's age, the game can be changed to one where the exchange of some words may be necessary and be discussed. Carol and Williams (1988) explain also how communicating and talking to toddlers, and we would add acknowledging important feelings and experiences, can prevent traumas in later life, or in Fahlberg's (1988) words 'can lead to psychological growth'.

Too many expectations too early can frighten children. Silences are often more appropriate as a way of reaching some of them. It is again only gradually that some children can be helped to put their thoughts and feelings into words. Having reached the child, which may take some time, an attempt is then made to help him or her look at their world and to sort out their feelings about what has been happening to them. Both painful and good things, such as good memories, may then be talked about remembering that once trust is established, most of the initiatives must come from the child.

A range of other toys, doll's houses, puppets, etc. can be used especially in the re-enactment of family life and in demonstrating/ illustrating to a very young child, the coming move from the birth family to another, e.g., to foster carers. Plasticine and play-dough are excellent mediums for emotional ventilation, particularly of anger. (Some of the activities suggested in the next chapter can be adapted for this form of individual work.)

Children up to their teenage years and possibly beyond, use play as a medium for expressing their feelings as well as for re-enacting events in their lives. West (1990) describes some useful practical ways of using play work and play therapy to communicate with children. As an example, play can be used as a therapeutic tool with children who have been sexually abused. Through its use, such feelings as fear, anger and sadness can surface and be discussed. Cipolla *et al.* (1992) discuss how play can give children an outlet to explore roles and feelings which can help the child to build 'feelings of autonomy, security and self-esteem'. Play can involve role-play, drawings, puppets, sand-play, cards and/or the adaptation of commercial games depending on age and level of understanding.

Therapy, in the form of free drawing, provides access to a child's preoccupations, provided there is no rush to interpret images and symbols. Understanding the child's world of preoccupations can help the worker to use reality-based talk and activities that could address such preoccupations without the need to interpret. Drawings involve play and also become the 'third' object which provides children with a means for testing reality and exploring new surroundings. Symbolic play and/or participation in activities can facilitate communication and help to clarify distortions and undue fears and concerns, assisting the child to feel more confidence and secure to re-invest in future relationships (Jewett, 1984).

Driver (1989), who studied drawings produced by children, claims that they can indicate the following specific feelings:

- the absence of any human figures within the picture, which symbolizes the child's fear of people.
- the absence of certain anatomical features. A person drawn without arms or hands may signify that the artist wishes someone to stop touching them or alternatively the child may be conveying a belief that they are not receiving any comfort or protection.

- a picture of a house, which often represents the body or self. If there are no windows or doors the child may be feeling trapped at home.
- male survivors of sexual abuse often draw a boy or a man with emphasized nipples. Such an exaggeration may stem from feeling upset or confused about gender roles.

There is often the misguided view that children should be protected from pain such as that involved in separation, divorce, illness or death. Bowlby (1969 & 1979) maintains from his studies on separation and attachment, that children can resolve losses just as favourably as adults, given the following conditions:

- have enjoyed a reasonably secure relationship with their parents or caretaker before the loss;
- receive prompt and accurate information about what has happened, and are allowed to ask all sorts of questions and to have them answered as honestly as possible;
- participate in any grieving, including funeral rites;
- have the comforting presence of parents or adults whom they trust and can rely on in a continuing relationship.

Honesty and the truth, within the child's capacity to understand and cope, are indicated, provided again that this is done with the help of a trusted and supportive person. The older child relinquished for adoption, or whose family has lost interest in them, will need help to separate emotionally from their parents, to 'mourn' their loss, and perhaps come to terms with the element of parental 'rejection' that is present in all such cases. Even if the parents are not necessarily rejecting, this is how it feels to the child.

Jewett (1984) suggests that young children get their understanding of life primarily through their senses, not through their intellects. She goes on to add that particularly with difficult and emotionally laden information, it helps to tie the news or information about painful events in their lives to a sensory or bodily connection. The information will sound more real to the child if it is conveyed through what they might have seen or heard, for example, 'you possibly felt that something was wrong with your mum when the doctor kept coming' or 'you often heard your mum and dad fighting and this could be scaring'.

In addition, Jewett comments that children process information differently from adults, and the way they process it changes as they get older. Initially, up to about the age of 7, children believe that their own thoughts, wishes and actions cause what happens to themselves and to other people. This is a form of 'magical' thinking, for example, 'my father left us because I kept wetting my bed', or 'my parents left me because I am bad'. The clear message that must be given to any child in such situations is that it was not their fault for what has happened, that it is not because they are bad or have been troublesome, and that nothing they could have done would have made things different. By about the age of seven or so children move on to concrete thinking which lasts until about the age of 12. During this stage the child thinks in terms of 'either/or', good and bad, and there is little ability to deal with subtleties or ambiguities. Things are either one thing or another.

Donley (1981) outlined what she called her 'ten commandments' about communicating with children. All of them are very relevant to what is being discussed here, but of particular importance are the following: avoid clichés in talking to children; assume that any child you are going to work with has some deep concern that has never been adequately understood or answered; understand from the beginning that children in care have been hurt; and be prepared to become a dependable, predictable and regular fixture in the child's experience.

THE MAIN TASKS INVOLVED WHEN MOVING CHILDREN

One of the initial tasks with children who are about to be moved or who have been moved, is that of assessment to enable matching between needs and foster carers' skills. Like observation, communication can aid assessment. Carse (1987), cites the example of a 12 year old who was admitted to care as an emergency after being locked out of the house by her father who then left for business. After initial hesitation, she found the confidence to play with a sand tray. In this she created a busy snow scene where 'no one seems to notice one another' and 'animals and people were all going home'.

Grimshaw and Summer (1991) (quoted by Sinclair & Garnett,

Private Communication, 1993) suggest that the most significant activities associated with assessment can all be regarded as preparation for decision-making. They go on to add that for informed decisions to be taken it is necessary to obtain the views of children and young people.

Fitzgerald (1991) outlines the following areas to be considered when assessing the child's circumstances and needs:

- a detailed chronological history of the child's experiences, including numbers and changes of carer and levels of physical and emotional care;
- a full and developmental history;
- a detailed history of the child's educational experience;
- full details of the circumstances and type of possible abuse experienced;
- a record of the child's own views and perspectives in relation to his or her own life, and how this was obtained, and
- a record of the parental views and perspectives in relation to his or her own life, and how this was obtained.

Fitzgerald goes on to say that time spent on consideration of these areas can pay handsome dividends when devising a 'treatment' plan.

Tasks before Moving into Foster Care

Children may move to foster care either directly from home or from residential care. As already pointed out, moving children from their familiar environment to a new one has been identified as being a most traumatic and distressing experience. Children between the ages of about six months and five years are even more vulnerable to such moves because they are not fully able to comprehend exactly what is happening to them.

Though many children can make successful re-attachments to new temporary or long-term carers, some of the trauma can linger for a long time. The way removal is managed, along with the quality of the subsequent care offered, could be decisive in whether or not the child overcomes the trauma and anxiety involved in the separation experience. Again, sometimes it may not be possible for the worker to undertake the preparatory tasks outlined below and they may have to be done retrospectively. It is also preferable for the preparatory work to be undertaken by the social worker who has already been known to the family and the child thus introducing at least some element of continuity and a link with the past. Children view social workers, like teachers, as very powerful people. As a result, they carry within them a mixture of hopes and fears about social workers.

The main preparatory tasks, shared whenever possible with the parents, include:

(1) preparation for the pending move offering explanations of why it is necessary and being aware and responding to unspoken fears, anxieties and preoccupations;

(2) explaining and discussing the nature of foster care (or residential care) and what it usually involves. Also discussing the plan and the fall-back plan, and what living with another family may entail;

(3) arranging for a meeting between parents and foster carers and, if everyone is satisfactory, arranging for the foster carers to meet the child;

(4) arranging a pre-placement visit to the foster carers and their children, while, in the meantime, a similar preparation of the foster carers and their children is taking place;

(5) discussing visiting arrangements, identifying at the same time personal items to accompany the children. Information is obtained about the children's routines, health, patterns of living, etc. provided by the parents for the foster carers;

(6) depending on the children's age, outlining their rights (and those of parents) preferably in written form; children also need to know how to complain, if things go wrong, and

(7) giving a specific date and time when the social worker will escort the children to their new home, in company with their parents, unless this is not possible.

MATCHING CHILDREN AND FOSTER CARERS

Like the assessment of foster carers, the matching of children to foster carers is far from being an exact science. There is a lot that still remains to be learned. There are few guidelines on how to recognize qualities in carers and equally how to identify children's exact needs. Nevertheless, we need to start with what is known and build on it. The idea of matching children with the skills of the carers receives some support from studies such as Borland *et al.* (1991) and Cliffe and Berridge (1991).

As part of the process, the concrete and intangible qualities in both the foster carers and the child must be considered, in an attempt to match needs and skills. For this, practitioners have to study carefully the child's assessment in conjunction with that of the carers. It would be inadvisable, for example, to place a child who lies or bedwets with a family who cannot tolerate such behaviour; or place a rather withdrawn child with an extrovert, boisterous family, an outgoing child with a rather quiet family, or a very demanding and needy child with a large family with young children. Similarly, some families are better than others in setting out limits which can be of particular help to the 'acting-out' child or those involved in delinquent behaviour. We are not saying that a disregard of what has been said above will not work, but the risks will be greater.

Smith (1988) gives the example of a family who placed a lot of importance on meals as a social occasion, yet when a girl of seven joined them, she showed her unhappiness by continued vomiting, including at meal times. The family members became more and more angry and the girl more and more unhappy.

Some important concrete matching criteria include the religious persuasion and wishes of the birth parents and/or racial, ethnic and cultural factors. Guidance notes to the Children Act 1989 on the subject emphasize

> . . . in the great majority of cases, placement with a family of similar ethnic origin and religion is most likely to meet a child's needs . . . Such a family is likely to provide a child with continuity in life and care in an environment which the child will find familiar and sympathetic . . . opportunities will naturally arise to share fully in the culture and way of life of the ethnic group to which they belong . . . Families of similar ethnic origin are also usually best placed to prepare children for life as members of an ethnic minority group in a multiracial society, where they may meet with racial prejudice and discrimination and to help them with their development towards independent living and adult life. (Department of Health, 1991, p. 11)

There is also emphasis on helping children 'to understand and to take pride in both or all elements in their cultural heritage and to feel comfortable with their origins' (Department of Health, 1991, p. 11). There is recognition that where it has not been possible to make a placement reflecting the child's race and culture, then ways must be found to find ways for providing links with the child's cultural and racial background. Family diversity and change have significantly increased over the last thirty or so years and so also have intermarriage and couple relationships between members of different ethnic groups. It would be unrealistic to expect that it will always be possible to match the multitude of variables involved. What should be aimed for is approximations, taking account of parental and children's preferences, wishes and feelings, along with past history and general circumstances.

This is not the place to debate the wider issues concerning transracial and own-race placements. However, if there is a limited place for transracial adoption, this is much less so in the case of fostering. In fostering, unlike adoption, the child in most cases is expected to return to their original family. Placing such children transracially and possibly with a family of a different cultural or ethnic background, inevitably exposes them to influences which can be very different from those of the family of origin. Return home could involve the child in significant re-adjustments, which may not be successfully accomplished. In other words, children will find themselves having to shed the customs, values and outlooks of their white foster families and once again begin to take on those of their birth families. Not surprisingly, one of us with experience in child guidance work, had examples of such children being referred to the clinic and who were confused about their racial, cultural and ethnic identity. Sometimes they would blame their parents for 'being different'.

Diana Smith, a young woman who had been transracially placed in foster care, commented on this point when addressing the 8th International Conference on Foster Care, held in Dublin in July, 1993, 'It is precisely because I am black that I experience things differently. Our cultures are bound up in who we are as people and if you ignore my blackness, then you ignore and deny me.'

Matching older children is usually different from matching younger ones. For a start, older children can express their wishes more clearly. Older children have a longer history of places, people and events which they, and we, will want to see continued for the sake of the children's identity, if nothing else. Few older children requiring placement in foster homes are also likely not to have any behaviour and/or emotional problems. The BAAF outline referring to matching in adoption, recommends that information to be used in matching should include needs and motivation, the ways in which children cope with stress, interests, values and family life experience, possible difficulties, loss and separation episodes, expectations and hopes for the future, ability to tackle various kinds of behaviour, and reliance.

Not only it is right and proper that the children and their parents should be consulted about fostering, but their views need to be given careful consideration. It is difficult to think of situations where an older child's wishes should be put aside. A positive preference for the contemplated move usually enhances the possibilities of successful outcome. However, we should equally be open to the possibility that wishes can change over time. As an example, some children and often parents, change their minds about fostering after they have the opportunity of meeting the would-be foster carers.

INTRODUCING CHILDREN TO FOSTER CARERS

Whether the young child is moving from the birth family to foster carers or from foster carers to adoptive parents, there have to be introductions and contacts established between the existing and the new carers. The first introduction, as Fahlberg (1981) suggests, should preferably take place in the child's own territory, where things and people are familiar, and where the child feels more secure. She goes on to add that the new carers should not force themselves on a child, but simply be there and talk with the current carers. They may bring several toys for the child to play with, eventually leaving one behind and taking the rest with them. Later on, when visiting the foster home, the child will find familiar toys.

To convey the idea of moving to new carers, the social worker, uses dolls and figures as well as houses to illustrate the move from one to the other. The idea of a new carer is introduced gradually before the foster parents take the child home. If the child is moving from foster carers to new foster carers or adoptive parents, the latter should spend some time in the foster home. As Fahlberg (1981) again points out, it is advisable that the new carers visit at different times of the day, so that they can get acquainted with the child's routine. If the child is very young, the new carers can be asked to handle, feed, change, or put the child to bed.

With both younger and older children, the parents' preparation of the child, and their attitude to the idea of foster care, can be crucial in how the child transfers from one family to the next. The same would apply if the child were moving from foster care to adoption. The foster carers have to be involved in the whole plan. Failure to include existing carers in the preparation, could result in unnecessary competitiveness and resentment. In the end, the child receives the same message from everybody, that is, that the move has been planned by all and is supported by all. It is suggested, that on the day of the move, the existing carers and the new ones do joint packing openly and, if possible, with the child participating. With somewhat older and more verbal children, the approaches described earlier can still be used. Words can be used more with the parents present to talk also about foster care and the move. They can explain that the move is meant to be temporary and that the social worker will keep in touch and arrange visits and that the parents will also be visiting (Fahlberg, 1981).

With older children, words will play a much bigger part in discussing and explaining the move and what it entails. Some of the research studies reviewed in Chapter 4 suggest that good preparation usually leads to the stability of the new placement and to fewer breakdowns. Previous experiences of separation will have left memories or their marks, some pleasant and some unpleasant. Explanations about the plans, visiting arrangements and length of stay will all be important. If time allows, again a first contact in the child's home territory for initial introductions is desirable. A subsequent visit to the foster home, possibly involving an overnight or a weekend stay, could be arranged before final arrangements are made.

INTO PLACEMENT

A fair number of placement breakdowns involving older children usually occur soon after children have joined their new family. In research terms we still do not know the relative importance of pre-placement preparation, support during placement and post-placement support. All three are important, but there are those who suggest that more time should be spent in supporting the placement once the child is placed, rather than being involved in lengthy preparations. Because there are so many unpredictable things that could happen to separated children and so many intervening variables, it is advisable to plan for all the tasks at the different stages to be carried out carefully and methodically.

Some children will settle into their foster family quickly and the latter may wonder where the problems outlined by the social workers have gone. This is not surprising. New patterns of family interactions and responses generate different reactions in the child. Some children will only begin to be their usual selves when they feel more secure in their new home. Other children, though, may be attention-seeking, withdrawn, abusive or troublesome. The withdrawn child may pose a threat to the competence of parents who expect quick returns and appreciation. Yet depressed feelings may be most appropriate when the child's whole psychosocial world is changing. Children may equally demonstrate testing-out behaviour, or, as is not unusual, repeat previous patterns of behaving and relating. (For further discussion on children's behaviour in new placements, see Cann, 1980.)

Foster families struggling to cope with difficult behaviours may need reassurance that they are handling the situation properly, or at least that it is not their fault. The entry of a child into a foster family will cause fundamental readjustment in patterns of communication, interaction and relationships. For example, the family's boundaries will have to open to include or accommodate the foster child. Not all behaviours and difficulties can, of course, be explained on the basis of changing interactions within the foster family. There are situations, however, when foster carers come to feel that their mixed feelings, guilt or anger about the situation are not normal. This can lead to fears about the possible failure of the placement. Katz (1979) suggests that such possible feelings should be explored and discussed prior to the placement, though it does not stop them from appearing again.

TASKS IN FOSTER CARE

A key social work aim with children who are in foster care is to help them to sustain and develop their identity and self-esteem to resolve possible difficulties, learn to socialize and to prepare them for their return home or the next move. The specific tasks which can be achieved through individual and group sessions include:

(1) continued discussions to further their understanding of what is happening to them and what the plans are;

(2) ensuring the inclusive nature of foster care by promoting the children's understanding about their origins, maintaining and promoting the links with their families and helping them to develop positive images about themselves and their background;

(3) starting a life story book as another means of working in this area, recognizing that the way we feel about ourselves affects our behaviour, way of life and expectations. We know from studies that many children in care do not feel very good about themselves and this can affect other areas of their lives. Some of the reasons for this, as McFadden (1992) also points out, may have to do with past experience, repeated separations, unhappiness and disappointments;

(4) discussing why some children may never be able to return home, though the links need not be broken;

(5) being aware of children's reactions to living in a foster home, including their reactions to contact with their birth families, and

(6) demonstrating that you value and respect them, including their race, culture and ethnicity.

There also has to be recognition that some teenagers in care may be gay or lesbian whose needs may require special attention.

Though groups have been found to be particularly useful with adolescents and teenagers, pre-adolescents can also make good use of such opportunities. Yet Shaw and Hipgrave (1989a) claim to have found no evidence from their study that group support to young people in foster care was used other than in 'a handful of schemes'. Fanshel et al. (1989) also regret the fact that so little group work is undertaken with children during foster care. Yet their research supported the view that group work was a useful resource, particularly with acting-out children and/or those who could not otherwise tolerate the intimacy of foster family life.

Euster *et al.* (1984) outlined the following programme for what they called their 'life skills group' for adolescents:

Session 1 Feelings and perceptions about themselves or of being fostered. (There are a number of different exercises described in the next chapter that can be used individually or in groups, to encourage, particularly adolescents, to explore such feelings.)

Session 2 Making friends – use of role play, games, puppets.

Session 3 Information about sex (and HIV and AIDS) – use of films illustrating reproduction, contraception, teenage pregnancy.

Session 4 Sexuality – the ability to discuss and clarify personal values as well as to explore feelings about sex and marriage and other issues, including same-sex partners.

Session 5 Personal and relationship problem-solving; communication skills, assertiveness skills, self-discipline and stress control.

McFadden (1992) describes how children in foster care can be helped to learn to listen to others and to control their tempers. She suggests the use of such means as role-play with specific situations, for example 'Your foster father tells you to do something that you really don't want to do: how do you respond? do you agree to do it? argue back? compromise? think about running away? do something else? if so, what? How do you respond when the class teacher says, "You have been late again and you will be in trouble if you do it again"?'

The following two examples also illustrate how individual work can be carried out with children in foster care taking account of their age and level of understanding. (For the case examples we are indebted to former students.)

The first case is that of a three-year-old boy who was fostered with his sister, aged two, following their mother's death of AIDS. The father, who had a drink problem, was unable to cope and had requested care. In spite of his young age, 'W' had a long history of separations, losses, abuses and neglect. 'W' presented a serious management problem to the foster carers because of his aggressive behaviour, his tempers and destructiveness. A day centre place was found for the two children while at the same time 'W's' social worker arranged to have weekly sessions at the centre with him to help him overcome some of his difficulties. These sessions lasted for about nine months; during this period the social worker used play, drawings and words to communicate with 'W' and to help him develop some trust and channel his anger and frustration differently.

A different example is that of a 14-year-old girl, 'D' who was placed with foster carers following conflict and acrimonious relationships with her family, particularly between 'D' and her stepfather. Besides relationship difficulties at home, 'D' was described as needing help in making and sustaining relationships as well as help around her sexuality. Alongside counselling and conciliation work in family sessions involving 'D' and her family, the social worker also undertook individual work with 'D'.

During the initial stages of the individual sessions, the worker tried to gain 'D's' co-operation and establish a more trusting relationship. This she did by inviting 'D' to visit places in her car, go swimming, which 'D' enjoyed very much, talk about life in the foster home and sometimes just sit and watch TV. Gradually, she introduced a number of practical exercises with the aim of developing 'D's' self-image and self-esteem, or focusing on topics such as alcohol, sexuality, HIV and AIDS and relationships. Using the exercise called 'snakes', 'D' charted important and significant events in her life offering prompts for discussion; this resulted in 'D' mentioning the time she was taken into care because of disagreements and fights at home. At a later session an exercise was used to obtain an idea of how 'D' perceived herself. The exercise consisted of a problem check-list and 'D' had to assign various attributes to herself from a group of cards and then, based on these, draw a picture. In this case 'D' identified that she did not always follow advice and did not like being told what to do. On another occasion she used the opportunity to talk about her father and such topics as relationships and alcohol abuse.

LEAVING FOSTER CARE

While the tasks described earlier concern children at any stage during their fostering there are also a range of tasks to be accomplished as preparation before leaving foster care. Yet preparation for leaving foster care should be a continuation of the preparatory work undertaken before entering care and foster care, and be part of the ongoing work. Exit from foster care could involve a return home or a move to a residential setting, adoption or independent living.

The criticism has often been made that much less attention is paid to the preparation of children returning to their own families compared to children moving to adoption or from residential care to a foster home. Research has established links between the amount and quality of preparatory and post-placement work undertaken with children, their families and carers, and the subsequent stability of the arrangements (Marsh & Triseliotis, 1993; Farmer & Parker, 1991).

McFadden (1992) identified a number of specific issues to be considered as part of the preparation and which can be carried out in groups or individually:

- *Choices when leaving the foster home*: discussion could be initiated by asking the young person(s) to list three important choices which form the basis for discussion.
- *How certain outcomes can be achieved*: e.g., getting a job, making friends, buying new clothes, being healthy.
- *How unpleasant consequences can be avoided*: e.g., getting into fights, unwanted pregnancies, saying 'no' to alcohol and drugs, avoiding HIV and AIDS, not going to prison.
- *Financial plans*: possible income and expenditure. An exercise could involve asking young people to choose a certain income on leaving foster care. Can they live on it? Will they have to save before leaving? How do you save? What do you spend money on now? Could some of it be saved? What choices can you make about money? How would you go about shopping on a notional sum of money?
- *What will it be like to select housing and furnish it?* How would you get best value? Sketch a one bedroom flat and furnish it. Choices must be made between different desirable things; will

some purchases have to be delayed? Where is the money to come from? What does sharing a flat involve? Discuss the negative efforts of running into rent arrears, big fuel bills or getting into debt.

- *Employment*: Introduce the topic of getting employment. Why work? What rewards are associated with work? How do you prepare for work? Ask each member of a group to list the kind of job they had experience of and the jobs they would like to seek; what were the choices based on? What do they like and dislike about the choices. Ask participants to identify their special specific skills or strengths for these jobs. How do you apply for jobs? Prepare for interviews? What does being an applicant for a job mean?

Nothing can obviously substitute for the actual experience of trying to set up a home independently, but advanced preparation can provide at least some sensitization to possible hazards (McFadden, 1992). A number of possible situations could be role-played, especially in groups

- a friend asks you for money though he/she has not repaid an earlier loan;
- how to say 'no' to a date or to unsafe sex;
- how will you raise the matter with a flat-mate, who does not help in keeping the place tidy?

Unlike many young people who may have the support of their families when they move to independence, those leaving care or foster care may have no one else to turn to besides the social services. The more fortunate ones may have the continued interest and support of their foster carers. Yet the availability of fall-back support can make the difference between success and failure. The most vulnerable teenagers leaving foster care and other forms of care, are those with no social base in life to fall back on. Part of the social work role is to identify the children with no such base and begin to construct one for them, well before the time comes to leave foster care.

The experience of young people leaving foster care and other forms of care, suggests that success itself is relative, with achievements, set-backs, new attempts, sometimes despair before some stability can be attained. To expect a different scenario would be courting only disappointment. Too much is often expected of young people leaving care or foster care, something not usually expected at this age from those whose families are still fully behind them. The following comment by a homeless young person typifies the situation: 'For me the experience of being homeless, not having a home, a family, a base to go back to has been rather like the calm before the storm and over again.'

KEY POINTS FOR PRACTICE

- Children find separations from their families and other familiar figures distressing. As a result, a lot of preparation is required to reduce their distress, unhappiness and possible feelings of rejection.

- Work with children and young people in foster care is necessary in helping them to deal with possible feelings about their situation and to contribute to planning about their future.

- Preparatory work for returning home, joining a new family or moving to independent living, contributes to the subsequent stability of the arrangements.

- The ability to communicate both verbally and non-verbally is a necessary skill required for carrying out the tasks identified above.

---

8 Facilitating Techniques for Working with Children in Foster Care

In the next pages a number of suggestions are offered, mainly in the form of practical exercises, that could be used to facilitate communication with children either at the individual or group level. The techniques can be adapted for use with other children within the care system who are not placed with foster carers.

FACILITATING TECHNIQUES FOR INDIVIDUAL WORK

Below are listed certain techniques grouped according to the main aims we have in mind when using them in direct work with children. Examples are then provided of the kind of games and exercises that can be used. Social workers need to bear in mind that we are giving only a few examples under each heading. They should also take hold of the principles involved and develop their own ideas to suit the needs of the individual children depending on age, level of understanding, disability, etc., as well as their own personality and skill levels. The techniques are grouped under the following headings:

1. *Communication facilitators*: These are techniques which mainly facilitate or aid the process of direct work.
2. *Nurture facilitators*: These focus on sensory experience, regressive forms of play and other behaviour.
3. *History and identity*: These are ways which mainly help children to focus on past events and people in their lives with the aim of sustaining a positive identity and self-concept.

4. *Behaviour awareness and planning facilitators*: Techniques which are used in order to help children to make conscious changes in their behaviour or, more precisely, to be conscious of making a change and to become involved in making plans for the future.

Communication Facilitators

One of the early tasks in work with children is to obtain enough information to assist us in arriving at an assessment of their needs and an understanding of their wishes and preferences. The information will come from a number of sources such as parents and other family members or care staff in residential establishments. Children themselves are a central source of information and, as Corrigan and Floud (1990) point out, the initial aim is to open communication and build trust. They suggest a number of exercises, games and drawings, lists of likes and dislikes, eco-charts, etc. Older children can also write down their views. The parents' and relatives' accounts are also obtained helping to create a profile of the child. Other sources are a flowchart, medical information, information from the school, perhaps using information from one of the various social adjustment tests (e.g., Bristol Social Adjustment Guide), observation of the child by a carer or an outsider, the social workers' description of the child and the impact of past changes on the child. Corrigan and Floud (1990) add:

> We use all this information to estimate the developmental age of the child, and where the child may be stuck; and we look at the child's intellectual stage, social behaviour, and emotional and moral development. We look at him or her as an individual with skills, hopes and fears. Has he/she any attachments to anyone? What sort of attachment? Who could give permission to this child to make a move or a change? (p. 29)

We have found it possible to differentiate still further under the heading of 'Communication' to talk about three types of communication facilitators: starters, barrier-breakers and discussion focusing games.

Starters
The first contact a worker has with a child is important and may set the tone for the work and relationship that follows. Starters are

'games' or arranged 'happenings' used mainly to 'pave the way', 'oil the works' or, as we say, 'break the ice', so as to make it easier to begin to communicate. For example, a child can be asked to draw themselves on a path leading from their home to the foster home adding who else they might like to come along, or could be asked to draw a picture in a provided photo-frame of a special person they would always like to remember while in foster care, or write down the people they would like to keep in touch with.

We can think of one case of a very unco-operative child where the worker and he began to communicate easily at the first meeting because the new worker had taken the trouble to learn that this 12-year-old boy was 'mad about football' and the worker arrived at their first meeting with a board game called 'World Cup Final'. He and the child had to learn the rules together! This is an example of an 'arranged happening'.

One piece of starter equipment we have sometimes found useful is an ordinary office filing-box (Fig. 8.1). This may be used in a variety of ways, but we started using the 'collective box' as we now call it, quite early in the process, in order to help children pass information about themselves to the worker. Most children will have some 'treasures' or photographs of themselves, or birthday cards or letters from loved ones, and if they have not, we are immediately presented with an opportunity of working with the child to obtain a collection. The idea behind the box is that the child builds up a collection of memorabilia and helps the worker fill up the box. It may be that this material forms the start of a collection of photographs etc. for making a life story book (see under 'History and identity' below) but in any case the fact of using a piece of equipment – a box – and having something specific to do, actually facilitates communication.

We always carry a collection of felt pens, paste, adhesives, pencils, rubbers and so forth so that the child may put their name (and maybe the worker's) on, or inside the box. Some children like to stick cut-out coloured pictures on the outside of the box.

Another example of a starter game is shown in Figure 8.2, called 'Getting to know you'. Here the worker and the child have a card each, marked out in squares. They each draw, in the squares, important people or things in their lives. They then 'play' on their partner's board, using dice and markers. When the marker lands on a square, which it does whenever one shakes the dice, the

Figure 8.1 An ordinary 'boxfile' used in preparation work.

Figure 8.2 'Getting to Know You' boards

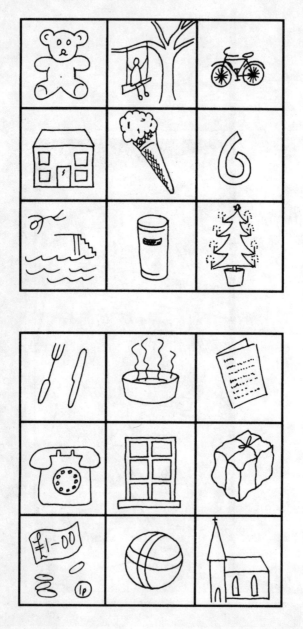

person who shook the dice and landed on the square can either ask the other player specific questions about the person or object in the drawing, or ask the other player to talk in general about the drawing. That 'game' was invented by a voluntary child care society, Familymakers' Home-finding Unit, England who have found it very helpful.

Barrier-breakers

With young children who find it difficult to talk about feelings or who may be shy, we have made use of a method devised by Vera Fahlberg ('Forest Heights Lodge' Clinic, Colorado, USA). This method employs a set of face-cards which has the same face expressing different moods. One face is smiling, the next card shows it crying, and so on (Fig. 8.3). When a discussion subject or an object, such as a photograph, is introduced we may ask the young child to point to the face that feels like he or she does when they see the photograph or think of the subject (angry, happy, sad, etc.). Figure 8.3a is another example on the same theme taken from Ryan and Walker (1985).

Another little gadget we designed is the slider (Fig. 8.4). The child and the worker can move a little panel or slide-window up and down a long card which has any desired number of subjects (or feelings, or names of people) written on it. The person whose turn it is to select the subject for discussion moves the slider window over the subject. It is best to design cards for individual children, or with the help of individual children. A third column could be added with a heading such as: 'Favourite Things/Happy Things' including phrases such as 'Favourite hits', 'Favourite stars', 'Favourite games', 'Things I'd like to do', 'Favourite dreams', 'I went to . . .', 'I love to . . .'.

On the following page are three lists we used on sliders with a 10-year-old girl. Subjects such as 'Mum being ill' were included as it was felt from previous work with her that this was an area of anxiety. In direct work with children we must be imaginative and prepared to design 'games' or adapt ideas to suit the needs of individual children.

Discussion-focusing

Clearly, some of the ideas already discussed, such as the slider, help to focus on subjects. We have used sets of discussion cards in

Figure 8.3 Face-cards used to help young children indicate their feelings.

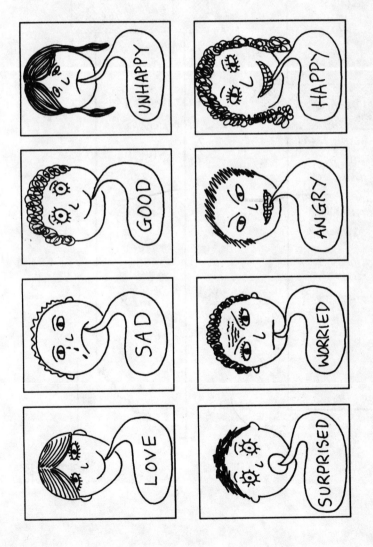

Figure 8.3a Helping the child to talk about feelings (from Ryan and Walker, 1988).

Figure 8.4 'Sliders' may be used to facilitate talk, and to direct talk.

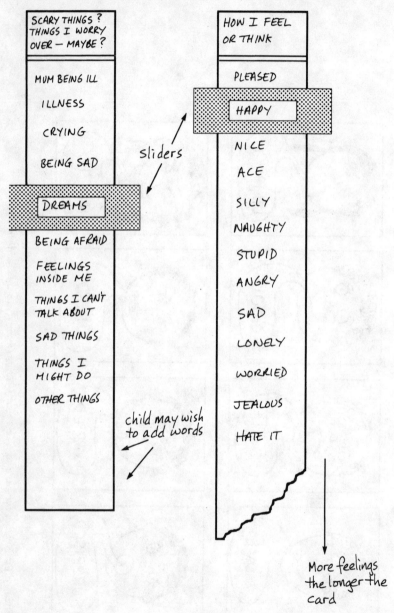

order to facilitate focusing. These cards can vary enormously. An easy way of making a set is to use plain white postcards. They may be used as they are or cut in half to make smaller cards. Starting, for example, with 12 cards, the worker can name four subjects (or draw a picture on each card to represent a subject) and the child can, if he or she wishes, name some subjects or draw pictures. Some cards are left blank for subjects which may crop up later. All the cards are then placed on the table or floor, and the child and worker take turns in choosing a subject. Both can therefore focus on what they wish.

Nurture facilitators

Although the techniques used here may appear to be very simple and the materials (paints, colour felt-tipped pens, bowls of water, sand, modelling clay, etc.) in common use in nurseries, nursery-schools and play groups, the use of nurture facilitators may be essential in the treatment of the child. It should also be noted that an extensive theory base applies to the use of these techniques. It is possible, here, only to introduce the subject.

Our experience with children appears to confirm the literature that their experiences of deprivation influence the emotional (affective), cognitive, motor and sensory aspects of development, and that often the children had either missed out on experiences which are normally required for the development of these aspects of personality, or their experiences had produced inhibitions or other pathological sequelae.

Some children need to be able to express themselves in painting (using large brushes and large sheets of paper). They need to re-experience colour, to experiment with colour. The same goes for sound, and other experiences. Some children are helped by water-play. We often start with a large bowl of water, with various containers and small 'dolls' that swim and dive, and some bubble-bath fluid. A child may blow down a rubber or plastic tube to make 'a million bubbles – look at them!' – with 'rainbows' or iridescent colours in them.

The nurture-facilitating techniques may include other forms of regressive activity. Much of the play we have described provides an opportunity (or an excuse) to regress. But we often give the child an opportunity to play with dolls and to 'feed' the dolls milk or orange juice from a baby-feeding bottle. Quite often a child will ask to have a suck from the bottle 'just to see what it is like'. Some children readily accept an opportunity to be bottle-fed even at nine or ten years of age.

Providing various forms of sensory experience, and allowing regression, appears to release tension and gives children an opportunity to make up for some of the experiential gaps in their lives. A useful book for the further study of nurture facilitators is *Windows to our Children*, Oaklander (1978).

History and Identity

Many children experience problems relating to self-identity, either because they do not know about their past (they feel they have no roots), or because they are carrying ideas and fantasies concerning their past, and these are emotionally upsetting and damaging to them. Discussing what they know about the reasons for coming into care and being in foster care, and who has told them what, can help to bring some clarity to their minds. Cards, each having a different reason for coming into care, can be used; the child is asked to select the ones most appropriate to their situation. The workers can also take the opportunity to comment that the child is not alone in their experience, that also many children are not responsible for what has happened and that it is not their fault. A group discussion around this theme can reinforce the individual work done.

Black and mixed-parentage children can be introduced to ideas about race and colour using pictures of black people and other images of black people. There is a range of books and exercises that could be used offering the children the opportunity to colour themselves, people like themselves, etc. Banks (1992) outlines a range of practical techniques for direct identity work with black children covering such areas as (a) altering the perception/social portrayal of blackness within the child's experience; (b) blackness as a positive aspirational goal; (c) the active joint discovery, appreciation and acclamation of the historical presence and achievements of black people; (d) highlighting, by discussion, the positive presence of black people on TV and also in films; (e) selection of children's books, posters, etc. with multicultural themes for discussion and appreciation of black people's existence in society; (f) active labelling to indicate the child's ethnic belonging through explicit statements, and (g) a black role-model in the role of therapist. It is recognized that the latter suggestion is rather controversial unless it can be justified on a child's specific needs.

Life Story Books

A life story book is an account of a child's life, family circumstances and environment in words, photographs, pictures, drawings and documents made by the child with the assistance usually of a social worker, or any other adult whom the child trusts. The life story book keeps children in touch with their past life and circumstances, helping at the same time to integrate this part of themselves with their developing personality. The idea of life story books developed from the research on origins carried out in adoption (Triseliotis, 1973). Life story books were seen as responding to the needs of children separated from their families, allowing them to know about their origins and equally about how they arrived at where they are now.

The life story book, through the discussion of facts, situations and people, conveys to the child a picture of his or her past and present, with the goal of preparation for the next move into the future. Within the framework of the past and present, uncertainties, hopes and fears about the future can be raised and discussed. The issue about a new family can be broached and explored, eliciting where feasible the child's own views and feelings. Such feelings and thoughts will affect the child's attitude towards new carers. Overall, the life story book, besides linking the child to his or her past, can also be part of the preparation before moving to a new, and sometimes permanent family. It is a common phenomenon now for children joining new families to carry with them their life story book and, increasingly, their video tape. It is our view that life story books should be prepared for every child in public care, irrespective of whether they are to return to their family, remain where they are in a residential establishment or foster placement, or move to another foster or adoptive home. (For more details, see Ryan & Walker, 1985 and 1993; Astrop, 1982, and the Northern Ireland Foster Care Association, *Life Books for Children in Care*, undated.)

Cipolla *et al.* (1992) identified four essential elements inherent in life story books, three of which are relevant to children moving to foster care:

1) *Exercises on the past*: These are concerned with events in the past and about the child's genealogical background.
2) *Exercises on the present*: This is achieved by reconstructing the child's self-image, identifying feelings and grieving for losses.
3) *Exercises on foster care (or adoption)*: The focus is on the actual process of the placement.

(The authors go on to suggest a fourth stage called 'disengagement work' in order that the child feels ready to move on to life in a new family. Though most children in foster care eventually return to their families, this aspect of the work is still relevant, especially if they are to move to a permanent new family.)

A life story book is not meant to be a mechanistic exercise to get over. Apart from the psychological and social meaning that it has for the child, making a life story book affords an opportunity for the social worker to get to know the child through working together. Collecting materials, documents, photographs, taking pictures, making drawings and recording facts are activities that bring social worker and child together and promote communication. The life story book becomes the 'third object' or the medium that can break the silence or enable communication to happen.

When the compilation of the book actually begins will depend on the child's readiness. The birth family may also actively contribute towards making the book. It is something that should not suddenly be imposed on a child, but be allowed to unfold gradually. In fact, it would be good practice to engage the parents in the preparation of material for the story book, preferably before the child moves to foster care. Once started, it can become a book to which additions are always made until the child moves to a permanent adoptive home or returns to their family.

With very young infants, the social worker takes the responsibility of collecting and putting material together until the child is old enough to contribute. Great sensitivity is required in checking with the child what should be recorded. The choice of words can be very important in conveying something about a particular event or happening.

As already pointed out earlier, an initial piece of useful equipment for starting life story books is an ordinary filing box, adding the child's name on the outside (see Fig. 8.1). Material from the collecting box can be used to construct the child's life story book. If material is missing then the worker, alone, or with the child, should try to gather it by visiting relatives, friends, the place where the child was born or previously lived. If the child is old enough to accompany the worker then this is an added chance for informal communication. A camera is always a good tool to take when visiting places connected with the child's past and present life. Gaps in the information will have to be made up accurately. The social worker may have to write to previous agencies or hospitals or children's homes to help obtain information to complete the child's background history. Significant people in the child's life, such as grandparents, former social workers,

Figure 8.5 Front page of life story book. The title could be written by child or worker, depending on age.

children's home staff, doctors or nurses may have to be visited to obtain first-hand information.

Information on the Child

Meaningful information on the child's early life would include: place and time of birth, weight and where he or she was taken after birth. This sets the pattern to chronicle the child's life stage by stage and especially the possible change of carers. The outside page of the life story book could say, for example, 'This is Peter's Story' (Fig. 8.5).

Figure 8.6 Example of a first inside page of a life story book

Photograph of the Red
Cross hospital where
Peter was born

Born: date

(The social worker may take
a photograph of Peter
outside the hospital)

Time: 8.00 p.m.
Weight: 3.5 kilos

The   Hospital   is   in
....

Liverpool

*This is a photocopy of my birth
certificate*

My birth parents' name:
....

......

Photocopy of
birth certificate

My birth mother:
Mary

....
My birth father:
Andrew ....

Figure 8.7 Example of a second inside page of a life story book

The first six months I
spent with my birth
mother at Byron Street,
No. 9 in Liverpool

Photo of me and my
birth mother

My birth mum was:
(physical description
of birth mother.
Special interests,
hobbies)

My birth father was:

(same as mother)

The map where Peter lived with his birth mother in the first six
months of his life:

The first inside page usually has information about the child's
circumstances of birth and early life, along with information on
the biological family, including grandparents, and any other meaningful relatives. Children born out of wedlock have fathers too, and
where they are not known, mothers should be encouraged to
provide information.

Peter's story could be continued, describing and illustrating why
Peter then had to leave his grandparents; the story follows the rest
of his life up to the present moment. Because events stretch over a
period of time, it is advisable to have a quick flow chart showing
briefly the various events in the child's life as illustrated in the flow
chart below (Fig. 8.9). This could be inserted on the first or
second page of the life story book as a quick guide to his life story.

The way the flow chart is used will depend very much on the age
and intelligence of the child, and other factors such as how much

Figure 8.8 Page 3 of Peter's life story book

The home where Peter
lived with his *birth mother*

```
┌─────────────────────┐    ┌─────────────────────────────┐
│                     │    │ From 6 months to 15 months  │
│                     │    │ Peter lived with his        │
│                     │    │ grandparents                │
│ (Peter may want to  │    │ Helen and Paul . . . because│
│ be included in the  │    │ his                         │
│ photograph)         │    │ mother emigrated to Canada  │
│                     │    │ and could not take him with │
│                     │    │ her because                 │
│                     │    │ of her circumstances. We    │
│                     │    │ know                        │
│ This is Byron Street,│   │ that she loved Peter.       │
│ No. 9.              │    └─────────────────────────────┘
└─────────────────────┘
```

The home where Peter lived with his *birth mother*

(Peter may want to be included in the photograph)

This is Byron Street, No. 9.

From 6 months to 15 months Peter lived with his grandparents *Helen* and *Paul* . . . because his mother emigrated to Canada and could not take him with her because of her circumstances. We know that she loved Peter.

Peter's Family Tree

Mum's Great-grandparents   *Dad's Great-grandparents*

Mike   Ann   not known
Taylor (aged 78)
(dead)

Grandparents   *Grandparents*
Helen   Paul   Sheila   George
(aged 51) (aged 54)   (aged 58) (aged 65)
died when   Cleaner   Retired
Peter was   Factory
15 months)   Worker

Children   (Nothing known about
                                                 father's brothers and sisters)

John   James   Mary (not married)   Nick
(aged 21) (aged 27) (aged 25)   (aged 30)
Van driver Mechanic (Peter's birth   (Peter's birth
Uncle   Uncle   mother)   father)

Peter

(Peter's Mum and Dad had no other children.)

Figure 8.9 Peter's Life Chart (flow-chart)

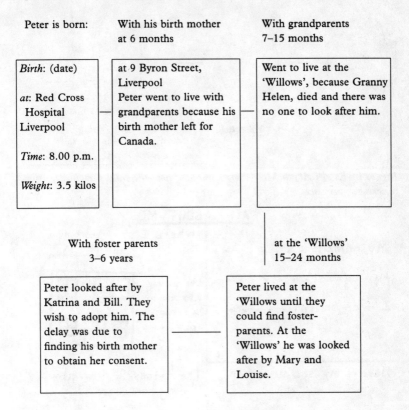

Peter is born:

With his birth mother
at 6 months

With grandparents
7–15 months

| *Birth*: (date)

at: Red Cross
Hospital
Liverpool

Time: 8.00 p.m.

Weight: 3.5 kilos | at 9 Byron Street,
Liverpool
Peter went to live with
grandparents because his
birth mother left for
Canada. | Went to live at the
'Willows', because Granny
Helen, died and there was
no one to look after him. |

With foster parents
3–6 years

at the 'Willows'
15–24 months

| Peter looked after by
Katrina and Bill. They
wish to adopt him. The
delay was due to
finding his birth mother
to obtain her consent. | Peter lived at the
'Willows until they
could find foster-
parents. At the
'Willows' he was looked
after by Mary and
Louise. |

in the worker's estimation the child already knows. Figure 8.9b is another example of personalizing the experience and Figure 8.10 another example of a flow chart.

We do not have to stick to dry old boxes. We may, for example, have a series of interesting shapes, and give them different colours, as in Figure 8.9a. Whenever possible the child would be encouraged to colour the shapes (watercolour or powder paints are best if you wish to write inside the shapes afterwards), and of course some children may like to choose the shapes or even to draw them in.

A lot more detail than we have shown here will go into the 'boxes' and the child and worker will talk about people and

Figure 8.9a. Life flow-chart using shapes (and colours)

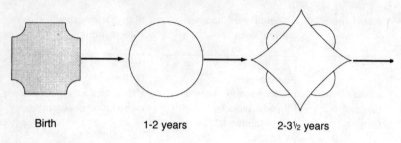

Birth   1-2 years   2-3½ years

Figure 8.9b. 'All About Me' – an example of how the child personalizes the fostering experience.

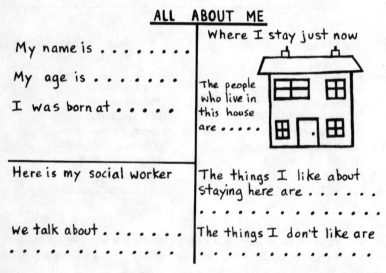

incidents and memories, and will try to correct possible wrong impressions and reinforce positive ones.

A further example which helps to clarify social and psychological aspects in a situation, and which assists identity formation, is what we would call the 'candle demonstration'. When using the candle demonstration we are making use of symbolism in order to clarify a situation, and express and share feelings about that situation. We use the candle demonstration in situations involving loss or

BIRTH

Various details of birth are given here including date, names of parents, place of birth, weight, length. Also names of child and siblings, child's home address etc.

0 – 1½

This child spent his first eighteen months with his mother and maternal grandparents. This section could show their names and where they lived. It could include people in the extended family and say why the child came into care

1½ yrs – 3 yrs

His mother was unable to look after him. This section names the foster parents who cared for him, and refers to other members of the household. Also looks at why the child moved.

3 yrs – 5 yrs

This period was spent in a childrens home. Talk about some of the staff. Can he remember them? Does he want to see them again? Did he like it? Where were his parents? Why was he there so long? etc.

5 yrs –

The basic flow chart is a series of boxes, as above.

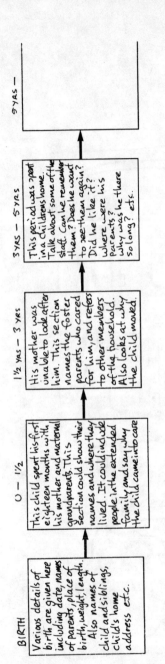

I AM BORN

MY NAME IS SUSAN

Born ......
at ......
Mums name ......
Dads name ...... me

AT TWO YEARS OLD

nana and me

Went to live with nana at ......

because ......

AT FIVE YEARS OLD

Went to live with Jane and Don Williams on a farm. The reason why I went was ......

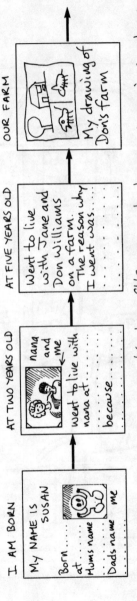

OUR FARM

My drawing of Don's farm

Many children like to use gummed 'Jolycraft' Squares which come in various colours, and then they can stick drawings or photographs on these squares.

Figure 8.10. Example of a flow-chart.

155

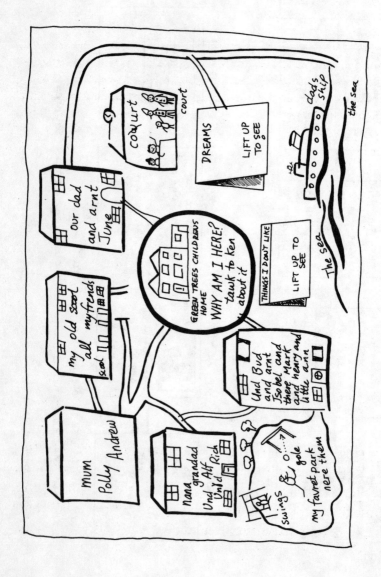

Figure 8.11 Example of 'Sociogram' or 'Eco-map' drawn by an eight-year old.

separation. Perhaps a previous caregiver has been 'lost' by separation, for example, a child hitherto cared for by grandparents who are now too frail to do so.

We light a candle for the child and explain that the flame stands for the love the child has for the previous caregiver. We move the previous caregiver's candle away, but explain that the flame (the love) has not gone out and still reaches the child, and that, similarly, the child's love still reaches the past caregiver. Then we bring two more candles which symbolize the 'new' parents (permanent foster carers or adopters) and we light flames for them symbolizing their love for the child. Now we light another candle for the child (put the child's two candles on a small dish together). This flame symbolizes the love the child has (or hopes to have) for the new

Figure 8.11a 'Snakes'

Imagine that the snake represents your life. Starting from your childhood can you think of the events, people, or places that were turning points for you. Mark these on the snake starting at the top. Also mark in things that were important to you at different times and show how these led to where you are now.

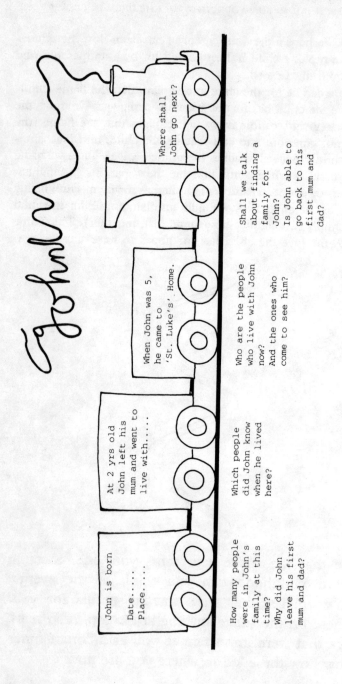

John is born

Date......
Place......

At 2 yrs old John left his mum and went to live with......

When John was 5, he came to 'St. Luke's' Home.

Where shall John go next?

How many people were in John's family at this time?
Why did John leave his first mum and dad?

Which people did John know when he lived here?

Who are the people who live with John now?
And the ones who come to see him?

Shall we talk about finding a family for John?
Is John able to go back to his first mum and dad?

Figure 8.11b The picture of a train helps young children in understanding the idea of moving.

Figure 8.12 'The Shield'

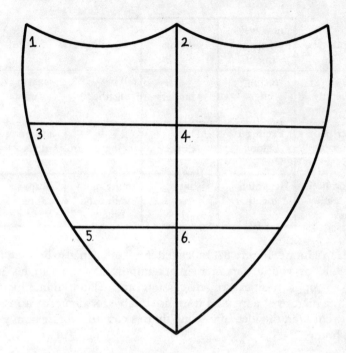

WRITE IN EACH BOX

1. The best thing that has ever happened to you
2. The worst thing that has ever happened to you
3. Others' views of you
4. A motto for you
5. Your hope for the future for the people you live with
6. Your hope for the future for yourself

family. We can show the child that because new loves (flames) have developed, the old ones do not have to be extinguished.

Figure 8.11 is another example of a 'sociogram' where an 8-year-old child is helped to express ideas about his relationships in his family, e.g. separated parents, his position in care and in the

Figure 8.12a 'Wall-building' – The shaded portions show the bricks which have been worked on.

Old memories	new ways of doing things	asking	cuddling	School
Sleeping	feeling angry	Manners	talking together	sharing tasks
Other people in my life	Feeling I belong	Dad's duties	being clean	accepting rules
Saying how we really feel	laughing together	sharing things	Being open with each other	Mum's duties

children's home. Figure 8.11a, called 'Snakes', can also be used for the child or young person to mark important events in his life offering opportunities for discussion and elaboration. Figure 8.11b, a picture of a moving train, is suitable for demonstrating to young children the idea of moving, in this case to a foster family or back home.

Behaviour Awareness and Planning Facilitators

Most children and young people enjoy self-completion exercises. These can offer the opportunity for discussing the situations when the behaviours or reactions occur, and perhaps to structure role-plays or games which offer the child the opportunity to respond differently. For example, Figure 8.12, the image of the shield, can be used in a number of ways to elicit difficulties, hopes and aspirations.

Another game we have found helpful in chronicling attitude and behaviour change, especially during a period of introduction to a new family, or during gradual rehabilitation to the child's natural family, is that of 'Wall-building' (Fig. 8.12a). The game is described by Pat Curtis (1983) and lends itself to variations. Children and young people who are moving into a new family

Figure 8.12b This checklist is useful in identifying possible difficulties.

	Quite a lot	Hardly ever	Never
I worry about my appearance			
I find it difficult to get on with others of my own age:			
I never do as I'm told:			
I ignore advice and do what I want:			
People criticize me a lot:			
People talk behind my back:			
I talk about others behind their back:			
I haven't got any friends:			
I find adults difficult to get on with:			
I don't like people in authority:			
I don't get on at school – with teachers: – with others:			
I get fed up:			
I am easily led by others:			
I don't get on at home:			

need to build a relationship with their new caregivers and the caregivers also share the task of building a good relationship with the child.

The bricks may represent relationship tasks, such as 'sharing things' or 'saying how I really feel'. They may represent attitudes which need discussing, such as 'accepting rules', or they may stand for little behaviour particles such as 'laughing together' or 'cuddling'. This concept of building (or adding-to) is helpful because the child does come to recognize that there is an effort, a task, and as we build up the bricks a feeling of achievement may also result.

As each subject is discussed, so a part of a brick (say a third or half) is painted in. When the worker feels the child has been able to satisfactorily cover the subject, the whole brick is filled in until, finally, the wall is complete. Figure 8.12a shows a wall being built; Figure 8.12b can be used to provide information around some of children's possible concerns about themselves and what others may think of them. Finally, Figure 8.13 is an example of an exercise that can be used to introduce the idea of talking about other families with children, pets, etc. The idea is to help the child to talk about these life experiences concurrently with the introduction to, and settling into the new family, or the rehabilitation to the natural family.

THE SPECIFIC USE OF GROUPS

Older children seem to find it easier to talk in a group of peers rather than in a face-to-face interview. The group process is generally meant to supplement the individual work which usually precedes and/or is going on concurrently with the group approach. The child's individual social worker usually introduces the idea of the group to each child, who can then consider participation. There may be situations where it might not be enabling for a child to participate, for example, a very destructive, or a very withdrawn child. More individual work may have to precede introduction to a group. The children's social worker may or may not be acting as a leader and co-leader. (For additional material on the use of groups see Triseliotis, 1988; Hoggan, 1988.) More specifically, groups can be used with the following aims in mind:

- to help them prepare for moving to a foster care family, returning home, or a move to a new family, e.g. adoptive;
- to help social workers get a better understanding of the children with a view to being more able to match them with foster carers;
- to help them understand the reasons for being in care;
- to help, particularly, older adolescents gain a greater understanding of what it will be like to live with foster carers;
- to help them explore relationships and ideas;
- to discover more constructive ways of coping with difficult situations they may face;

Figure 8.13 Introducing the idea of foster families with siblings, pets, etc.

Brothers and Sisters.
Some families have lots of
children 2, 3, 4 or more!

Some families have just one child

Some families have pets too!

WOOF

MIAOW

- to help them be more positive about themselves and their families, and
- to raise any unresolved issues they may have about their lives

Below we provide an example of how a group can be used to help children move from a residential unit to foster care. It is customary to hold five to six meetings and the number of children ranges from four to six. A larger group may impede the more individual attention required when games and exercises are used. The aim is also to keep a balance between male and female children. The content of most groups varies between those who put the emphasis on activities such as games, role-play and exercises, and those who keep a balance between these and talking about feelings. The group can meet weekly or every fortnight. The leader and co-leader usually meet beforehand to plan the kind of things the group would be doing, the management of the group and the handling of the feedback process from role-plays and exercises.

The following is a typical example; the example can be adapted to take account of the children's age.

Session One: Following introductions and an explanation about the group's objectives – what the group is going to be doing and why – a game is introduced to break the ice, the main objective being to help the children get to know each other a little more and to relax. The game is called 'name-game'. The children are told that a good way to get to know each other is by asking questions, like television interviewers do. The leaders show the children cards which have questions such as 'What is your age?', 'What is your favourite TV programme?', 'Which school(s) have you attended?' and then instruct the children how they would go about interviewing each other. The children are usually slow to begin with and can be very quiet and uncertain about what they are supposed to do. With a little encouragement they usually begin asking questions of each other and of the leaders, and get into the spirit of the game. A second game that can be used alternately with the TV interview is to hold the interview over the telephone. They could also interview the leader and co-leader. These games can make everybody feel more relaxed and begin to talk about why they are there.

Session Two: This session is labelled 'How we find foster families'. Not only young children but adolescents too can have some strange ideas about how families are found. A game is introduced called 'Find a Foster Family' which is used to stimulate discussion about where foster families come from. It involves a pack of cards with serious and light-hearted suggestions about how families are found, e.g. 'We advertise on TV or in newspapers', 'We put up posters in Post Offices', or 'They have to support Arsenal', or 'We drag them out of pubs'. The children have to decide which cards are jokes and which are realistic. They can debate between themselves which cards are right and wrong. This game can lead through to wider discussions about foster carers.

This session could also be used to encourage children to write posters about themselves, their likes and dislikes, good and bad points, favourite TV programmes, etc.

Session Three: This is called 'Family Jigsaw'. This is a game designed to get you and other children to think about what kind of family they might like to live in. They are asked to choose pieces of the jigsaw puzzle, and told that while they put the pieces in the different puzzles they should try and think hard about how they would fit in, if they were a piece of the jigsaw. This game makes many children and young people become involved. Subjects raised could include: 'families with cars', 'families with grannies', 'single parents', 'brothers and sisters', 'houses with gardens', 'Small families' and 'big families'. In one group a girl wanted a mum and dad with no other children to take her and her brother. Another one was uncertain.

A further session may be necessary to explore with the children such questions as how to fit in a foster home, following rules about living, negotiating around rules, learning about the routines of the foster home, issues about privacy, owning things, etc. For example, if foster carers are warned not to get attached to the children what is the appropriate behaviour for the children?

Session Four: This session is called 'True Feelings' and participants play a game called 'Feelings Bingo'. Each person has a card with a number of feelings written on it. The leaders then read out individual 'feeling' cards with words such a 'sad', 'nice', 'excited', 'hurt', 'mixed-up'. The person who has the feeling card out on their card, is expected to talk about the time they felt like that. One girl said, when the word 'sad' was read out, that she felt like that when 'she thought about her mum'. She then related a long story about her and her mum. The 'feelings bingo' game involves the children in talking about some very painful and personal feelings.

Some children could find it very difficult to talk about such feelings.

Session Five: This could be used to encourage the children and young people to explore their past and become more aware of their current situation. (It can also be linked to the individual work done with life story books.) Two exercises can be used for this. One is mapping the children's family tree, that is, the mapping of different members of their families, and which part of the family they belong to. This can help the children to clarify further in their minds their origins. The second exercise, an eco-map, encourages the children to draw maps showing where they are now, who else lives there, which school they go to, significant people in their lives, etc.

Session Six: The session concentrates on what living with a foster family may mean and how it may be different from living in a children's home. Different family compositions are discussed and the children explore the making of rules in families and how agreement can be made between young people and their foster carers about expectation and rights. A game of 'snakes and ladders' can be redesigned to include both positive and negative things which happen in families and the possible adjustments to be made.

Sessions can be added, and the games or exercises adapted to suit the circumstances. There is no blueprint on what the content should be. A session, for example, could be devoted to talk about 'our own families', 'what we think of them' and whether 'we will be allowed to talk about them with our foster carers'. The sessions outlined above could equally be described as somewhat over-structured, perhaps not allowing the development of greater inter-action and the full sharing of concerns and anxieties. Leaders and co-leaders need to keep this in mind, and continuously think of new ways of making children feel safe in the group so that they participate more freely.

KEY POINTS FOR PRACTICE

- A combination of activities and talking can be used to facilitate communication with children and young people, either individually or in groups.

- Talking and activities in the form of exercises and play can be used for preparing children and young people for entering care, while in care or as preparation for leaving care.

9 Working with Families Towards Re-unification

With few exceptions, as already pointed out previously, the ultimate aim of foster care is the reunification of the child with the birth family. The principles of reunification have been seen as part of the continuum which starts with preventive services within the household, uses away services such as temporary foster care when necessary, and eventually works towards the restoration of the child to his or her family. The provision of a range of home and away services have as their main aim the preservation of the family. All these efforts rest on the assumption, supported in most cases by research, that families are good for children.

The tasks for the social worker involved in reunification work are three-fold: to promote and sustain the links between the child and family, particularly through consistent visiting; to prepare the family to have the child back; and to provide post-restoration support to the family in order to maintain the home placement.

MAINTAINING THE LINKS

Studies suggest that one of the best predictors of reunification is the maintenance of the links between the child and his family (Aldgate, 1977; Millham *et al.*, 1986). It could be argued that it stands to reason that those parents who are interested enough to keep contact with their children in foster care are also those most likely to have them back. This may be so, but social workers have it in their power to encourage and support all parents in a number of ways, and not only those who are already interested, to keep the links with their children. The Children Act 1989 not only expects social workers to encourage contact but to promote it. To avoid drift in care or foster care, a named social worker has also to be designated. He or she will also try to ensure the implementation of decisions reached in consultation with parents.

The groundwork for maintaining the links between children and their families is something that usually starts before the child moves into foster care. Again research studies have shown that most children who enter care are well-known to the social services beforehand, though the actual admission frequently occurs as an emergency (Packman, 1986; Millham *et al.*, 1986). Emergency admissions raise issues about preparation, but parents and children need to be prepared against such a possibility without waiting until the last moment. Smith (1993) recognizes the difficulties involved when and if such work has to be carried in the face of hostile and angry parents. Parents whose children are accommodated on a voluntary basis in local authority care, usually feel less threatened and resentful towards social workers. In contrast, those whose children are removed through the courts usually feel more antagonistic. The social worker can only recognize and accept such feelings, demonstrating also concern for the child and the child's future.

Assuming that the relationship between the social worker and the family is based on the principles of partnership, as outlined in the Children Act 1989, subsequent work can be built on this. Partnership is about consultation before decisions are made and ongoing sharing of the tasks in hand. In other words, partnership is about giving families a voice to share in decisions made about their children. Though partnerships between social worker and parents will never be equal, nevertheless it is a move in the right direction. Commenting on the nature of this relationship Tunnard (1991) remarked that

the essence of partnership is sharing. It is marked by respect for one another, role divisions, rights to information, accountability, competence and value accorded to individual input. In short, each partner is seen as having something to contribute, power is shared, decisions are made jointly, and roles are not only respected but are also backed by legal and moral rights. (p. 27) (See also Marsh & Triseliotis, 1993.)

Early reservations about foster care on the part of some parents, and older children, are not unusual. However, we have known many parents and children change their minds after meeting the foster carers and being glad for it later. Smith (1993) quotes Atherton (1986) who points out that there is no reason to assume that parents will automatically know what placement with foster carers involves 'or what may be expected of them whilst their child is in care or in order for their child to return home as soon as possible'. Parents may have all sorts of misconceptions about fostering and varying degrees of guilt, anxiety and suspicion about foster parents looking after their child. They may also have read in the papers or seen on TV stories of foster carers wishing to keep their foster children. Social workers should tell parents about the preparation, training and role of foster carers; reassure them about the adequacy of care, and deal with often unspoken worries that foster carers will usurp their place in their child's life and affections.

PRE-FOSTERING PREPARATORY WORK

When it is becoming clear that the children may have to be accommodated in foster care, even though sometimes foster care may be preceded by a short period in residential care, the social worker will begin to discuss with the parents what foster care usually involves. A joint decision is aimed for, though differences can sometimes exist. In the case of older children their preferences and views have also to be seriously considered, which is one of the few rights they have in law. At the same time the parents are encouraged to talk to their children about both the possibility of a move or the certainty of a move to another family.

A few days before the move is made, specific foster carers are identified and discussed with the parents and children. Following this, parents and foster carers meet and if everything seems to be going well, they can be introduced to the children. An advance visit to the foster carers' home is then paid by both the parents and the children. Finally, a time is arranged when the children will be moved and parents, children and social worker go to the foster home. Such planning and skills are extensively used when children are placed from residential or foster care with adoptive families and they are very appropriate also when moving children from their families to foster carers. It may be an idea to be aimed for but seeing parents, social workers and foster carers working together is of value to the child and to the stability of the placement.

Atherton (1993) makes the point that besides shared decision-making and joint preparatory work, families also need to have easy access to three types of information.

The first is specific to their child and would include their address and telephone number; knowledge of what their living, including sleeping, arrangements look like; what school their child is attending; what other activities they are involved in; who their friends currently are; what their current interests are, and what sort of television, films, music, clothes they like. It is so easy to omit what can seem like small, insignificant details and yet such information is essential if families are to participate knowledgeably in planning for their children's futures. It is equally essential if families and children are to have enough 'currency' of conversation to maintain and strengthen their relationship.

The second is general information about child care law and local agency policy and practice. For example, a number of authorities have given the guide *Your Child and Social Services* (published by Parents Aid, Harlow) to each family using the care system.

The third type of information families need concerns the records kept by the local authority. Families need to feel confident about the work they do with professionals; they need to feel that views are shared and that professional opinions are not withheld. They need access to their files. Most local authorities now have a policy which opens up client records to some extent, although there are important differences in the ease with which users can see material on their files. Some authorities have highly restricted access, while a few have promoted even greater openness by using shared recording methods.

In Chapter 2 reference was made to the need and value of contracts which can set out the respective roles, responsibilities and obligations of each party, that is, parents, social workers and foster carers. The former Boarding-Out Regulations required that foster carers are furnished with specific information concerning a child who will be placed with them and to enter into an agreement in writing concerning the child. To avoid misconceptions about the nature of the placement, the contract should include the agency's plans for the child and the arrangements for contact. Smith (1993) adds that 'even with thorough assessment and preparatory work, foster carers can become confused about their role if they are unsure about social work planning and the part which they are expected to play in this' (p. 174–75). This is where the contract can again provide the needed direction about expectations, role and tasks.

The point was made earlier that frequent contact between parents and children in foster care, preferably through regular visiting, is usually a good predictor for the child's return home. Based on a number of studies (Aldgate, 1977; Fanshel & Shinn, 1978; Millham *et al.*, 1986), the following factors, in line of importance, have been found to contribute to increased contact:

- Parents believe contact valuable
- Attitude of caretakers positive
- Children's reactions positive
- Placement in children's home (This highlights the extra efforts required to promote visiting and contact for children in foster care.)
- Child over 5 years old at reception into care
- Early social work encouragement.
- Placement within one hour's journey.

Contacts are not only important because they are a signal of early reunification, but they also convey messages to the child. As most forms of separation are experienced by children as a form of loss and often of rejection by parents, visits convey to the child something about their worthiness in the eyes of their parents. Children are also able to observe directly the acceptance of their family by the foster carers and vice versa, thus reducing conflicts of loyalty. In addition, positive contacts and links have a direct effect on the child's well-being and self-image (Weinstein, 1960; Millham *et al.*, 1986) and discourage idealization and fantasizing on the part of the child.

Parents may be discouraged from visiting or keeping in touch with their children for a number of reasons. Some of the main ones are listed below.

Financial Difficulties

Visiting, especially if the foster placement is at some distance, may involve the parents in considerable effort and additional expenses such as transport costs, the costs of baby-sitting or child-minding, and the bringing of gifts. Though local authorities are empowered to pay the expenses of parents visiting children, Woodman (1982) found that only two of the twelve parents in her sample group said that they ever received travel expenses and one of them said that the expenses received did not cover the full cost of travel. Similar findings were noted by Aldgate (1977) and Thoburn (1980). Furthermore, when children are in care for more than eight weeks, the parents lose their entitlement to child benefit. A number of parents told Aldgate that they stopped visiting because they could no longer afford to take presents. Carers, whether acting as foster carers or working in residential establishments, may also pass explicit or implicit judgements on visiting parents and relatives that can be off-putting. Besides travelling, there is usually no reimbursement for other expenses. Wearied and over-harassed parents, who may already be feeling depressed, guilty and inadequate for separating from their children, can easily give up in the face of adversities.

Believing that Contact is Valuable

One of Aldgate's findings was how unaware some parents were of how important they were to their children. They thought that they commanded their children's love and respect only when they brought them large presents. Though social workers use explanation and social education when preparing new foster families, this does not seem to have been seen as necessary for birth parents. Such form of education and explanation could help them understand why they are important to their children.

The Attitude of the Foster Carers is Positive

As already mentioned, parental visiting may also be affected by the attitude of the foster carers, depending on how 'inclusive' or 'exclusive' they are of the birth family. In other words how welcoming they are to parents and how well children are prepared and made to feel that they are not being disloyal to the foster family by wanting to see birth parents and siblings. Foster carers have to be prepared not to see the child's parents as a nuisance or as being upsetting to the child.

Foster carers who enter fostering with an 'exclusive' attitude are, of course, much more likely to be off-putting to the natural family. Yet, as we have already seen, the child's welfare and self-image may also depend on how the birth parents are viewed and treated by the foster family. Aldgate (1977) again found a relationship between negative attitudes towards birth parents by foster carers and decline in the frequency of contact. Equally Woodman (1982) commented that the dissatisfaction of the parents in her sample was linked to perceptions of a hostile attitude on the part of the caretakers. More encouragingly, the professionalization of foster carers seems to have fostered a more positive attitude on the part of foster carers towards parental visiting and generally much greater inclusiveness of the family of origin (Triseliotis, 1980).

Suitability of Physical Arrangements

Lack of privacy and lack of opportunities to see their children alone was one of the criticisms made by parents to a number of researchers (Thorpe, 1974; Aldgate, 1977; Thoburn, 1980; Woodman, 1982). Parents told Aldgate that it was important for them to see their children separately for three reasons: 'It helped retain the relationship between parents and child; it enabled parents to ensure that children were well looked after, and most importantly, it made parents feel that they had a valued and trusted role in their children's care' (p. 445).

Smith (1993) recognizes the difficulties sometimes faced by parents when access visits are arranged in the foster carer's home and adds that if other preparatory work has gone well and foster carers are actively working with natural parents towards rehabilitation, contact in the former's home might well be appropriate and with some thought and imagination can be fun and mutually rewarding. However,

> contact must be arranged sufficiently frequently, taking into account the child's age, and at a venue where both parent and child can feel relaxed and able to enjoy each other's company. Social workers should pay explicit attention to this matter and discuss it with parents, foster carers and the child if he or she is old enough to express a view. (p. 174)

Though there are situations when visits have to be under super-vision, for example, when a parent has a history of harming the child, nevertheless in most cases this is unnecessary.

Children's Reactions

Children's reactions to parental visiting have often been given as one of the main reasons why foster carers and/or social workers terminate contact between parents and children. Kline and Overstreet (1972) recognize that by virtue of the problems in the family that brought about the separation, some visits could lead to stress in the children. Equally some children can feel misled and betrayed by their parents' inconsistent visits and unrealistic promises, or become distressed and burdened by the parents' unpredictable or disturbed behaviour. Some parental visits can leave the child anxious or confused, and he or she will need help to understand the parents' predicament. At the same time most children, even separated and sometimes rejected ones, think well of their parents and are ready to make allowances for them.

Distress following a visit is not necessarily an indication of unhappiness and a reluctance to have more contact on the part of the child. In other circumstances, we would have been glad to see the child express feelings compared to indifference. Sometimes practitioners, in order to buy peace with the foster carers, may collude in the exclusion of the birth family. The child needs to perceive the worker and the foster carers as sympathetic to the parents, and expects all three to be working together for a return home.

What has been said so far about working towards the foster child's reunification and keeping the links with the parents, does not rule out the fact that on occasions parental visits may have to be limited, or even stopped altogether, if shown to be detrimental to the child. The impact of parental visits and their meaning to the child have to be monitored and understood and if necessary regulated accordingly. Parents are sometimes disturbed or very rejecting or abusing, and the child may have to be protected at least until the situation changes. It would be irresponsible also to assume that visiting is always good for the child.

Being sensitive to the children's reactions and, when they are old enough, listening to their views can help practitioners decide what to do about some visits. Stopping visits, for example, because the parents are unable or unwilling to have the child back, and because we hope to place the child for adoption, are not good reasons. If the visits are of emotional significance to the child, then adoption with contact may be one of the solutions. The positive value of contact is now generally recognized, even in adoption, so there is no need to hold back permanency plans on behalf of the child.

Finally consistency and predictability are not characteristics of some birth parents, but visits can equally become less of a problem and less acrimonious if they are planned for and outlined in the agreement between foster carers, social workers, parents and child (where the latter is of an age to understand). Setting down procedures, and even times or days, can be helpful to both sides. Obviously, foster carers cannot be expected to be always available for unplanned visits, and parents cannot be expected to enter complex negotiations each time they plan to visit their child. A fair amount of explaining and educating may also be necessary so that parents can grasp the importance of their visits. For example, though children may show disappointment, it is not the presents that matter, but the parents' presence. Social workers can also explain that, with the passing of time, children inevitably get more attached to their carers which would make reunification more difficult.

PREPARING THE FAMILY FOR RE-UNIFICATION

The idea of restoring children to their parents from foster care mainly dates from the implementation of the Children's Act 1948. Like all new ideas it took many years before it began to permeate social work and child care practice. Until recently, research showed that even when the idea of restoration was present, not enough was being done while the child was away to support the parents to overcome possible difficulties that were present and prepare them and the child for the latter's return. The studies suggested that either social workers neglected work with the family following the usually hectic period of admission or that such neglect followed after an initial period of visiting and contact. Consistent work with the parents involving planned restoration work apparently diminished or petered out, especially if the case dragged on (Aldgate, 1977; Millham *et al.*, 1986). Fisher *et al.* (1986) and Farmer (1992) also found that most children's exits from care were unplanned and unprepared and were often initiated either by parents or young people in care. Yet we would not contemplate moving a child to a new family without adequate preparation of all parties. Separation will have inevitably given rise to feelings and created new circumstances that will require discussion and exploration.

Around 50 per cent of children who enter local authority care/accommodation each year return home within six months but for the rest restoration is a much slower process. Almost 40 per cent continue being in care after two years (Millham *et al.*, 1986). It is assumed that more intensive restoration work with the family will help to reduce the percentage of long stays considerably. According to Millham *et al.* (1986), the main reason for two-thirds of the children continuing in care after a year is fear of abuse, neglect or injury. Assessing and deciding on the right time for a child's return home is a highly-skilled job. Farmer and Parker (1991) found that about one-fifth of the children returned home were reabused.

Some parents, especially those whose children are accommodated for a short period, may need little help, encouragement or support to begin to prepare to have them back. Yet even these families may need some support to deal with their feelings of loss; they may need help to keep the contact and to begin to plan for the home-coming. Other parents, especially those in whose case the child was looked after because of abuse, neglect or acrimonious relationships, may require more consistent help over the difficulties that necessitated care in the first place. Parents should also know from the start what it is they have to do or in what ways they have to change, in order to have their children back. Expectations of parents should feature in the plans and in the agreement between parents and social worker, which is also required by the Children Act 1989. However, care plans and agreements are of little value if used mechanically rather than as a tool for good practice.

Changes required of the family could fall into any one of the following categories or a combination of these:

- improvement of the physical conditions and general environment;
- recovery from illness, for example, mental illness or alcohol abuse;
- improvements in parenting to reach acceptable levels such as in the areas of physical care, affection, stimulation and encouragement. (With the children away this may be more difficult to assess except from visiting and the occasional return of the children home.)
- changes in attitudes towards the child, for example, where rejecting or punishing attitudes prevailed, including the elimination of possible abuse.
- the resolution of difficult or acrimonious relationships between parents/step-parents and children.

However consistent and supportive social workers prove to be, they will not always be able to resolve all difficulties. They may be aiming to achieve 'good enough' conditions rather than idealistic ones. Failing this, rehabilitation from foster care may eventually have to be with other relatives or adoption and, in the case of teenagers, towards independent living with all its hazards.

In the attempt to effect change in the areas outlined above, the social worker will aim to identify who are the significant people to work with. For example, would it be the family as a whole, specific members of the family, a grandparent or a combination of these? The focus of attention may also have to shift sometimes to take account of new developments. Another variable to consider is who *can* change, in order to concentrate efforts in that direction. Clear, specific goals within the family's capacity are jointly identified and where necessary broken down into achievable parts. Smith and Corden (1981) demonstrate from their research how a task-centred approach proved productive with the majority of families who were facing both concrete and relationship difficulties. Part III of the Children Act 1989 sets out a range of services that could be made available to families going through a crisis and requiring support. The same types of human and physical resources and strategies can also be used to support families to resume the care of their children from foster care or other forms of care. (See also Marsh and Triseliotis, 1993.)

Some families are likely to be experiencing heavy environmental and personal pressures generating great stress for them. Many of the families whose children come into care are either one-parent or reconstituted families. Long periods of poverty, disadvantage and adversity will have contributed to many of their difficulties. At other times such difficulties may interact with attitudinal problems to create what may appear to be intractable difficulties. Being unemployed and on benefits for long periods of time can lead to social isolation, homelessness, lack of support, poor health, loss of self-esteem, apathy, powerlessness and feelings of marginality. Child care need can also be generated through the misuse of alcohol or drugs and of other behaviours. These can operate as both cause-and-effect influencing environmental behaviours, including the care of children.

As the families will have been known to the social worker before the child went into foster care, it is assumed that different approaches may have been tried to prevent unnecessary separations. Of course the child being away may be part of the plan to avoid the breakdown of the family in the long run. However, with the child away a new assessment and planning will be necessary to take account of the new situation. Any one of a number of models can be used to re-assess, jointly with the family, what needs to be done and how. A systemic framework can be one such model because, in spite of drawbacks, it pays attention to personal, family, environmental and concrete issues. Both instrumental and affective needs can be considered and intervention can address practical, environmental and family problems as part of a single package, though the timing for each may differ. Experience, supported by research (Sainsbury, 1975; Miller & Cook, 1981; Smith & Corden, 1981; Marsh & Triseliotis, 1993), suggests that the following strategies, singly or in combination, may be found appropriate in addressing some of the difficulties:

- Increasing concrete resources, where needed, to help reduce stress. This can be achieved through information giving, education, advocacy, negotiating on behalf of the family where necessary, protection against homelessness, debt counselling, access to legal aid and linking families to a power base such as self-help groups to become their own advocates, for example, learning how to claim benefits or gain access to other resources. According to Woodman (1982) parents of children in care were glad for the help they had received in the form of legal or welfare rights advice.

- Where needed, provide help and support in managing resources and in planning. Managing on very little for long periods of time is bad enough, but it is even more difficult under conditions of anxiety and of possible apathy.
- Helping families to maximize the use of day centres, drop-in centres, health centres, respite services, libraries, schools, etc. Confidence and self-esteem could be enhanced by becoming involved in the running of such services.
- Encouraging family members to improve existing skills or to learn new ones such as house and finance management or how to handle the children. For example, parents can be taught behavioural techniques about rule-making within the family or about setting limits to children's behaviours, including how to say 'no' when necessary and how to praise. Behavioural techniques appear to give parents the feeling of being in control which helps to increase their confidence. Similarly some parents may need help in controlling impulses which could have harmful consequences. Family members with alcohol, drug, mental health or physical illness may need support to obtain suitable treatment.

There are times when parents or other family members will want to vent feelings, consider choices, reflect on situations or debate issues as individuals, couples or as a family. It is, however, the demonstration of continued support in areas of practical living and management that usually create the atmosphere within which personal issues and relationships can be brought up and discussed. Feelings towards the child in foster care or any other child in the family or towards a spouse can then be examined too. For example, many adolescents are accommodated in foster care because of difficult relationships at home. Return home is often ruled out before such difficulties are at least partly resolved. Family groups, meetings and conciliation skills seem particularly suited to the exploration of strained relationships between older children and their families.

One study (Hardiker *et al.*, 1989) identified the following skills deployed by social workers in work with one family whose children were taken into emergency foster care.

- the use of intensive, task-centred methods over a short period, e.g., behavioural work, brief marital counselling,
- working with the father as well as with the mother,
- interprofessional co-ordination with a variety of colleagues and agencies and
- explicit division of labour between the social worker, family aide and home help.

These skills and methods were underpinned by a strong value base, that is, recognizing and supporting the parents' own informed choices and reinforcing their self-esteem. The services used included:

- social work (individual counselling, marital counselling, decision-making, child-care planning, co-ordination);
- the family aide and the specialist home help undertook practical help, support and advice, and behavioural work with the children;
- a specialist health visitor, a health visitor and a school nurse each visited fortnightly;
- a Mencap worker visited regularly;
- the two younger children attended a Mencap day nursery and playgroup;
- Section 1 money (as was then known) was used to finance the weekend, and to buy some equipment
- a DHSS grant was obtained to buy decorating materials, and
- a day nursery was found for the children. (Hardiker *et al.*, 1989, p. 137)

POST RE-UNIFICATION SUPPORT

One of the main lessons to be learned from the placement of children with new families is the importance of preparing the placement and of providing post-placement support. In other words, the stability of the placement largely relies both on the quality of the preparatory work undertaken and of the amount of post-placement support made available to the new families, sometimes over a 24-hour period. New families are given clear messages that they can get in touch almost at any time of crisis. Yet it is not certain that such clear messages are given to birth parents before or after they have their children back.

Research evidence supports the importance of this kind of work for the maintenance of the placement (Cautley, 1980; Berridge & Cleaver, 1987; Nelson, 1985; Yates, 1985). Important learning and new skills have been developed through this work that could be transferred to the preparation of children and their families before reunification and to providing support following the child's return. Some of the work with the family while the child is away, and identified in the previous section will usually have to continue and new forms of support provided to take account of the return. Preparation for return was found by Farmer and Parker (1992) to diminish the possibility of breakdown following return home. The skills and knowledge identified for use when moving children to new families, could easily be transferred to work with children returning home and for supporting them while there. (See Thoburn et al., 1986; Triseliotis, 1988; Hunter 1989.)

Post-return support can come in different forms. It could be in the form of practical services such as day care, holidays, respite facilities and baby-sitting, especially for very demanding children. It can also be in the form of individual or family counselling about ways of handling issues or difficult behaviour or mediating in disputes. Hill et al. (1988), referring to new families, adds that usually a variety of sources and types of support is needed from social networks, other parents, social work agencies and other professionals. They go on to add that

> some prefer to confide in their own parents, sisters or brothers; others in close friends; yet others in social workers. Different kinds of practical, social and supportive/counselling help are required because some families have multiple needs and also because what suits one person may not be available or appropriate for another. (p. 18)

Macaskill (1985) refers to relief care; discussions with other parents, special leisure activities, medical and educational facilities and befriending of the children by volunteers. Ideally, she comments, such help should be close at hand, accessible and well-timed.

Experience from the placement of children in new families suggests that one of the most valued forms of services is having access to a person or persons who can be consulted when a crisis is on and if necessary turn up. The ability of social workers to respond quickly during crises encourages parents to persevere and try to find a way through, particularly in the case of adolescents where disputes are not unusual. Families may also have to be linked to specialist services, for example, for speech, educational, medical or psychiatric facilities. In the study carried out by Hill *et al.* (1988), top of the parents' list were respite/relief care, more information about the child, counselling/psychiatric help and financial aid. Somehow we seem to be more prepared to assist, either in cash or in kind, new families who take on children with special needs rather than birth parents whose children return to them from care. The authors end with the comment that 'adequate and well-timed provision of two basic commodities – information and money – could have made life for some families more tolerable and thereby enhanced their parental satisfactions and capacities, with ultimate dividends for the children' (p. 23).

Perhaps the amount of help and support required by families whose children return from foster care has been underestimated because the children are returning, after all, to their own families. Apart from help to adjust to each other again, it is not often that the reasons which necessitated separation in the first place disappear by the time the child returns home. Past difficulties could also be rekindled and relationships take a turn for the worse if not mediated.

Farmer (1992) identified two distinct groups of children returning home either from residential or foster care. One group were younger children who had been accommodated or in care for reasons of abuse, neglect or family breakdown. The second was of adolescents who had either offended, truanted or were beyond their parents' control. The placement back home for the latter group was more likely to break down compared to the first group. Many of the difficulties for which they were initially removed reappeared again. The researchers strongly urge continued support to all families who return home to prevent the breakdown of the arrangement or further abuse. They viewed a child's return home as a major transition often requiring renegotiating relationships and roles at home and school. In most cases, both the children and their families had changed in significant ways. Apparently once the 'honeymoon' period was over children tested out and showed their distress in a number of ways such as 'defiance, temper tantrums, clinging behaviour, jealousy and nightmares. Practical help on how to deal with these behaviours was needed, as well as reassurance that such difficulties were to be expected' (p. 11). The authors add that the most heavily-used resource in support of placement was social work time, aided by the use of day care services in the case of three-quarters of the children who were under five. Sometimes a family aide was deployed at the start of placement. One of the important findings of the study was that cases in which there had been continuous social work involvement following the child's return home were more likely to be successful than those which suffered from periods when cases were not even allocated.

KEY POINTS FOR PRACTICE

- Birth families are very important to children

- The central concept of fostering is its temporariness, the ultimate aim being the child's re-unification with his family.

- Maintaining the links, mainly through visiting, between parents and children in foster care is the best predictor of re-unification.

- Parents may need considerable support, in the form of resources and/or counselling to enable them to have their children back.

- Return home has to be planned and followed by support to help maintain the arrangement.

- Many of the skills developed in the placement of children with new families, could be usefully transferred to families when they are reunited with their children.

References

ADAMSON, G., *The Care-takers*, London Bookstall Publications, 1973.

ALDGATE, J., 'Identification of Factors Influencing Children's length of stay in care', PhD Thesis, University of Edinburgh, 1977.

ALDGATE, J. and HAWLEY, D., 'Helping foster families through disruption' *Adoption and Fostering*, **10**: 2, 44–49, 1986.

ALDGATE, J., HEATH, A. and REEVES, C., 'The education of children in and out of care', *British Journal of Social Work*, **19**: 447–460, 1991.

ALMAS, T., 'After Recruitment: putting the preparation and training of Asian foster carers on the agenda', *Adoption and Fostering*, **6**: 3, 1992.

ANDERSON, L.M., 'A Systems Theory Model for Foster Homes Studies', *Child Welfare*, **61**: 1, 37–48, 1982.

ANDERSON, W., *Children rescued from pauperism or the boarding-out system*, Edinburgh, 1871.

ARGENT, H. (ed.) *Keeping the Doors Open; a review of post-adoption services*, British Agencies for Adoption and Fostering (BAAF), London, 1988.

ASTROP, J., *My Secret File*, Puffin, London, 1982.

ATHERTON, C., 'The Importance and Purpose of Access' in Family Rights Groups (ed) *Promoting Links*, Family Rights, London, 1986, pp. 11–19.

ATHERTON, C., 'Reunification: Parallels Between Placement in New Families and Reunifying Children with Their Families', in MARSH, P. and TRISELIOTIS, J., eds, *Prevention and Reunification in Child Care*, Batsford, 1993.

AUDIT COMMISSION, *The provision of child care: Final report*, HMSO, 1981.

BANKS, N., 'Techniques for direct identity and work with black children', *Adoption and Fostering*, **16**: 3, 19–24, 1992.

BARNARDO'S SPECIAL FAMILIES PROJECT, Edinburgh, *A Professional Fostering Scheme*, Progress Report 1, 1981.

BAYLISS, B., 'Who care for carers? – Helplines', *Foster Care* **73**, March 1993.

BEBBINGTON, A. and MILES, J., 'The supply of foster families for children in care' *British Journal of Social Work*, **20**, 197–220, 1990.

BIESTEK, F.P., The Casework Relationship, Allen and Unwin, London, 1961.

BERRIDGE, D. and CLEAVER, H., *Foster Home Breakdown*, Basil Blackwell, Oxford, 1987.

BLOM-COOPER, L., *A Child in Trust*, Brent Borough Council, 1986.

The Boarding-out of Children Regulations, HMSO, 1955.

BORLAND, M., O'HARA, G. and TRISELIOTIS, J., *Permanency Planning and Disruption in Lothian Region in Adoption and Fostering*, Scottish Office, Central Research Unit, Edinburgh, 1991.

BOSWELL, J., *The Kindness of Strangers*, Penguin, London, 1991.

BOWLBY, J., *The Making and Breaking of Affectional Bonds*, Tavistock, London, 1969.

BOWLBY, J., *Attachment and Loss*, Vol. 1: 'Attachment', Hogarth Press, London, 1979.

BRIAND, N., 'Kids in care don't go to college', *Independent*, 11.4.91.

BRITISH AGENCIES FOR ADOPTION AND FOSTERING, *Working Together*, British Agencies for Adoption and Fostering (BAAF), London, 1989.

BRITISH AGENCIES FOR ADOPTION AND FOSTERING, *Recruiting Black Families*, BAAF, London, 1991.

BROWN, J., 'Foster parent support group in a rural area', in TRISELIOTIS, J., ed., *Group work in adoption and foster care*, Batsford, 1988.

BRITISH AGENCIES FOR ADOPTION AND FOSTERING, *Communicating with Children*, training pack, British Agencies for Adoption and Fostering (BAAF), London, 1991.

BRYANT, B., 'Special foster care: a history of rationale', *Journal of Clinical Child Psychology*, 10: 1, 8–20, 1981.

CAMPBELL, C. and WHITELAW-DOWNS, S., 'The impact of economic incentives on foster parents', *Social Service Review*, 61: 599–609, December, 1987.

CAMBRIDGESHIRE SOCIAL SERVICES DEPARTMENT, *Support foster care scheme: A practice manual*, 1990.

CANN, W., 'Maintaining the Placement', in TRISELIOTIS, J., ed., *New Developments in Foster Care and Adoption*, Routledge Kegan Paul, London, 1980.

CAROL, J. and WILLIAMS, P., 'Talking to Toddlers', *Community Care*, 31.3.1988.

CARSE, C., 'A Search for Meaning of Loss and Transition in Art Therapy with Children', in DALLEY, T., ed., *Images of Art Therapy*, Tavistock, London, 1987.

CAUTLEY, P.W., *New Foster Parents: The First Experience*, Human Sciences Press, New York, 1980.

CAUTLEY, P. and ALDRIDGE, M., 'Predictors of Success in Foster Care', University of Wisconsin – Extension, 1974.

CHAMBERLAIN, P., MORELAND, S. and REID, K., 'Enhanced Services and Stipends for Foster Parents: Effects on retention rates and outcomes for children', *Child Welfare*, 71: 5, 38–401, 1992.

The Children Act, Guidance and Regulations, Vol. 3, 'Family Placements', HMSO, 1989.

CIPOLLA, J., MCGOWN, D. and YANULIS, D.B., *Communicating Through Play*, British Agencies for Adoption and Fostering (BAAF), London, 1992.

CLIFFE, D. and BERRIDGE, D., *Closing Children's Homes*, National Children's Bureau, London, 1991.

COLTON, M., *Dimensions of Substitute Child Care*, Avebury, Aldershot, 1988.

CORRIGAN, M. and FLOUD, C., 'A Framework for direct work with Children in Care', *Adoption and Fostering*, **14**: 3, 28–32, 1990.

CURTIS, P., 'Involving children in the placement process', *Adoption and Fostering*, **7**: 1, 45–47, 1983.

DANDO, I. and MINTY, B., 'What Makes Good Foster Parents', *British Journal of Social Work*, **17**, 383–400, 1987.

DAVENPORT-HILL, F. and FOWKE, F., *Children of the State* (2nd edition), Macmillan, London, 1889.

DAVIS, E., KIDD, L. and PRINGLE, K., 'Child sexual abuse training programme for foster parents with teenage placements', Barnardo's North East Division, London, 1987.

DAVIS, S., MORRIS, B. and THORN, J., 'Task Centred Assessment for Foster Parents', *Adoption and Fostering*, **8**: 4, 33–37, 1984.

DAWSON, R., 'The Abuse of Children in Foster Care', Summary Report, Ontario Family and Children's Services of Oxford County, 1983.

DEANE, J., 'Foster families feel the pinch', *Newcastle Evening Chronicle and Journal*, 16.5.91.

DEPARTMENT OF HEALTH AND SOCIAL SECURITY (DHSS), *Foster Care: A Guide to Practice*, HMSO, 1976.

DHSS, *Social Work Decisions in Child Care: Recent Research Findings and their Implications*, HMSO, 1985.

DEPARTMENT OF HEALTH, *Statistics from 1976 to 1991*. HMSO.

DEPARTMENT OF HEALTH, *The Care of Children. Principles and Practices in Regulations and Guidance*, HMSO, 1989a.

DEPARTMENT OF HEALTH, *Handbook of Guidance to the Boarding-Out Regulations 1988*, HMSO, 1989b.

DEPARTMENT OF HEALTH, *Foster Placement (Guidance and Regulations)*, Consultation Paper No. 16, The Children Act 1989, HMSO, 1990.

DEPARTMENT OF HEALTH, *The Children Act 1989. Guidance and Regulations*, Vol. 3, 'Family Placements', HMSO, 1991.

DEPARTMENT OF HEALTH, *Children and HIV: Guidance for Local Authorities*, HMSO, 1992.

DERBYSHIRE AND NOTTINGHAMSHIRE COUNTY COUNCILS AND THE SOUTHERN DERBYSHIRE AND NOTTINGHAMSHIRE DISTRICT HEALTH AUTHORITIES, *Report of the Inquiry into the Death of a Child in Care*, October 1990.

DEVON COUNTY COUNCIL, *Evaluation Report on Partnership in Alternative Care for Teenagers*, Devon County Council, 1981.

DONLEY, K., *Opening New Doors*, BAAF, London, 1981.

DOWNS, C., 'Foster Families for Adolescents: the healing potential of time-limited placements', *British Journal of Social Work*, **18**: 473–487, 1988.

DRIVER, E., 'Through the Looking Glass', in DRIVER, E. and DROISEN, A., eds, *Child Sexual Abuse; Feminist Perspectives*, MacMillan, London, 1989.

ELTON, A., 'Working with Substitute Carers', in BENTOVIM, A., ELTON, A., HILDERBRAND, J., TRANTRER, M. and VIZARD, E, eds, *Child Sexual Abuse Within the Family*, John Wright, London, 1988.

ENDLESTEIN, S., 'When Foster Carers Leave Helping Foster Parents to Grieve', *Child Welfare*, **60**: 7, 467–473, 1981.

ERIKSON, E.H., *Childhood and Society*, Pelican, 1967.

EUSTER, S., WARD, V.P., VERNER, J.G. and EUSTER, G., 'Life Skills Groups for Adolescent Foster Children', *Child Welfare*, **63**: 1, 27–36, 1984.

FAHLBERG, V., *Helping Children When They Must Move*, British Agencies for Adoption and Fostering (BAAF), London, 1981.

FAHLBERG, V., *Fitting the Pieces Together*, British Agencies for Adoption and Fostering (BAAF), London, 1988.

FANSHEL, D., *Foster Parenthood*, University of Minnesota Press, 1966.

FANSHEL, D., FINCH, J.S. and GRUNDY, J.F., 'Foster Children in LIfe – Course Perspective', *Child Welfare*, **68**: 5, 467–78, 1989.

FANSHEL, D. and SHINN, E., *Children in Foster Care*, Columbia University Press, New York, 1978.

FARMER, E., 'Restoring Children on Court Orders to their Families: Lessons for Practice', *Adoption and Fostering*, **16**: 1, 7–15, 1992.

FARMER, E., and PARKER R., *Trials and Tribulations: Returning Children from Local Authority Care to their Families*, HMSO, 1991.

FISHER, M., MARSH, P., PHILLIPS, B. and SAINSBURY, E., *In and Out of Care: The Experiences of Children, Parents and Social Workers*, Batsford, 1986.

FITZGERALD, J., 'Working with children who have been sexually abused', in BATTY, D., ed., *Sexually Abused Children*, British Agencies for Adoption and Fostering (BAAF), London, 1991.

FREEMAN, M., *Children, Their Families and the Law, Working with the Children Act*, MacMillan, London, 1991.

GEORGE, V. *Foster Care*, Routledge and Kegan Paul, London, 1970.

GRAY, G., 'The Training of Foster Carers', M. Phil. thesis submitted to the University of Sheffield, 1992.

GODWARD, P., 'Paid Fostering', *Foster Care*, **65**, March, 1991.

HAMPSON, R.B. and TAVORMINA, J. 'Feedback from the experts: a study of foster mothers', *Social Work*, 108–112, March, 1980.

HARDIKER, P., EXTON, K. and BARKER, M., *Policies and Practices in Preventive Child Care*, School of Social Work, University of Leicester, 1989.

HARTMAN, A., 'Diagrammatic Assessment of Family Relationships', *Social Work*, 1978, **59**: 10, 465–76.

HARTMAN, A., *Finding Families*, Sage, London, 1979.

HAWKINS and SHOTTET, *Supervision in the Helping Professions*, Open University Press, 1989.

HAZEL, N., *Fostering Teenagers*, National Foster Care Association, London, 1990.

HILL, M., HUTTON, S. and EASTON, S. 'Adoptive parenting – plus and minus', *Adoption and Fostering*, **12**: 2, 17–23, 1988.

HILL, M., LAMBERT, L. and TRISELIOTIS, J., *Achieving Adoption with Love and Money*, National Children's Bureau, London, 1989.

HOGGAN, P., 'Attitudes to Post Placement Support Services in Permanent Family Placement', *Adoption and Fostering*, **15**: 1, 28–30, 1991.

HOGGAN, P., 'Preparing Children, for Placement Through the Use of

Groups' in TRISELIOTIS, J., ed. *Groupwork in Adoption and Foster Car*, London, Batsford, 1988.

HOLLIS, F., *Casework: A Psychosocial Therapy*, Random House Press, New York, 1964.

HOLMAN, R. *Trading in Children*, Routledge and Kegan Paul, London, 1973.

HUNTER, A., *Family Placement: models of effective partnership*, Barkingside, Barnardo's, Batsford, 1989.

HUTTON, S., 'An Independent Adopters Support Group', in TRISELIOTIS, J., ed., *New Developments in Foster Care and Adoption*, Routledge and Kegan Paul, London, 1988.

JACKSON, S., *The Education of Children in Care*, University of Bristol, 1983.

JENKINS, S. and NORMAN, E., *Filial Deprivation and Foster Care*, Columbia University Press, New York, 1973.

JEWETT, C., *Helping Children Cope with Separation and Loss*, Batsford, 1984.

JONES, M.B., 'Crisis of the American Orphanage, 1931–1940', *Social Service Review*, **63**: 4, 613–629, 1989.

KADUSHIN, A., *Supervision in Social Work*, Columbia University Press, New York, 1985.

KATZ, L., 'Older Child Adoption Placement; A Time of Family Crisis', in CHURCHILL, S.R. *et al.*, eds., *No Child is Unadoptable*, Sage, London, 1979.

KIRK, D., *Shared Fate*, Collier, Macmillan, London, 1964.

KLINE, D. and OVERSTREET, H., *Foster Care of Children: Nurture and Treatment*, Columbia University Press, New York, 1972.

KNAPP, M., and FENYO, A., 'Efficiency in Foster Care: Proceeding with caution', in HUDSON, J. and GALAWAY, B., *The State as Parent*, Kluwer Academic Publishers, 1989.

KNOWLES, M., *The modern practice of adult education from Pedagogy to Androgyny*, Cambridge Book Company, 1970.

LINDSEY, C., 'Consultations with Professional and Family Systems in the Context of Residential and Fostering Services', in CAMPBELL, D. and DRAPER, R., eds., *Application of Systemic Family Therapy: the Milan approach*, Grune and Stratton, New York, 1985.

LITTNER, N., 'The art of being a foster parent', *Child Welfare*, **57**: 1, 3–12, 1978.

LONDON, L., 'Do All the Family Want to Adopt?', MSc dissertation, University of Edinburgh, 1992.

LONDON CHILD CARE FORUM, *Non-financial support for foster parents*, 3rd draft, 1988.

LOWE, K., *Teenagers in Foster Care*, National Foster Care Association (NFCA), London, 1990.

LOWELL, R.B., *Adult Learning*, Croom Helm, London, 1980.

MACASKILL, C., 'Who should support after the Adoption?', *Adoption and Fostering*, **9**: 2, 21–25, 1985.

MACASKILL, C., 'After Adoption', *Adoption and Fostering*, **9**: 1, 45–49, 1985.

MACCASKILL, C., *Adopting or Fostering a Sexually Abused Child*, Batsford, 1991.

MACLEAN, K., 'Towards a Fee-Paying Fostering Service', *Adoption and Fostering*, **13**: 3, 25–29, 1989.

MARSH, P., 'Contracts and the Beckford Case: Lessons for Foster Care?', in *In Whose Trust*, National Foster Care Association (NFCA), London, 1988.

MARSH, P. and TRISELIOTIS, J., *Prevention and Reunification in Child Care*, Batsford, 1993.

MCAULEY, C. and KELLY, G., 'Long term foster care in Northern Ireland', Paper presented at the 8th International Foster Care Conference, Dublin, July 1993.

MCFADDEN, E.J., *Preventing Abuse in Foster Care*, Eastern Michigan University, 1984.

MCFADDEN, E.J., *Fostering the child who has been sexually abused*, Michigan Department of Social Services, 1986.

MCFADDEN, J., *Push for Youth Goals*, National Foster Care Resource Centre, Michigan Univ, 1992.

MILLER, J. and COOK, T., eds., *Direct Work with Families*, Bedford Square Press, London, 1981.

MILLHAM, S., BULLOCK, R., HOSIE, K. and HAAK, M., *Lost in care*, Gower, 1986.

MINUCHIN, S., *Families and Family Therapy*, Harvard University Press, 1978.

NAPIER, H., 'Success and failure in foster care', *British Journal of Social Work*, **2**: 2, 187–204, 1972.

NATIONAL FOSTER CARE ASSOCIATION, *The Challenge of Foster Care*, NFCA, London, 1988.

NATIONAL FOSTER CARE ASSOCIATION, *A Problem Shared*, NFCA Training Pack, NFCA, London, 1990a.

NATIONAL FOSTER CARE ASSOCIATION, *AIDS and HIV: information for foster carers*, NFCA, London, 1990b.

NELSON, K.A., *On the Frontier of Adoption*, Child Welfare League of America, New York, 1985.

NISSIM, R., 'Who cares for carers? Practical support', *Foster Care*, 23 March 1993.

NOBBS, K., and JONES, B., 'Tread with Care', *Community Care*, 26–27, 9 June 1988.

NORTHERN IRELAND FOSTER CARE ASSOCIATION, *Life books for children in care* Undated.

OAKLANDER, V., *Windows to our Children*, Real People Press, 1978.

O'HARA, G., 'Developing post placement services in Lothian, *Adoption and Fostering*, **10**: 4, 38–42, 1986.

O'HARA, G., 'Placing Children with Special Needs. Outcome and Implications for Practice', *Adoption and Fostering*, **15**: 4, 24–30, 1991.

PACKMAN, J., *Who Needs Care?*, Blackwell, Oxford, 1986.

PARENT'S AID HARLOW, *Your Child and Social Services, Parent's Aid*, Harlow, undated.

PARKER, R., *Decision in Child Care*, Allen and Unwin, 1966.

PARKER, R., *Away from Home: A History of child care*, Barnardo's, London, 1990.

190

PARKER R., WARD, H., JACKSON, S., ALDGATE, J. and WEDGE, P. *Assessing Outcomes in Child Care*, HMSO, 1991.

PARLIAMENTARY PAPERS 176, *The Boarding-Out of Pauper Children in Scotland and in certain Unions in England*, 1870.

PASSMARK, L.L., 'An anatomy of foster parenting: tasks and concomitant knowledge, skills and attitudes with implications for foster parent education', Dissertation Abstracts International, Kansas State University, Vol. 40 (6A), PhD Thesis, 3163, 1979.

PASZTOR, E. and BURGESS, E., 'Finding and keeping more foster parents', *Children Today*, March/April, 1982.

PAYNE, C., and SCOTT, T., *Developing Supervision of Teams in Field and Residential Social Work*, London, NISW Papers No. 12, 1982.

PRICE, H., 'Foster parents switch councils in pay protest', *Independent*, 12 April 1992.

REDGRAVE, K., *Child's Play*, Boys' and Girls' Welfare Society, 1987.

RHODES, P., 'Charitable vocation or "proper job"? The role of payment in foster care', *Adoption and Fostering*, **17**: 1, 8–13, 1993.

RHODES, P., *Racial Matching in Foster Care*, Avebury, Aldershot, 1992.

RICKFORD, F., 'Squaring Roots', *Social Work Today*, **23**: 27, 15–17, 19 March 1992.

RICKFORD, F. 'Fostering with pride', *Social Work Today*, **23**: 37, 12–13, 28 May 1992.

RICKFORD, F., 'Endangered Species', *Social Work Today*, **24**: 5, 12, 24 September 1992.

ROWE, J., CAIN, H., HUNDLEBY, M. and KEANE, A., *Long-term Foster Care*, Batsford, 1984.

ROWE, J., HUNDLBY, M., and GARNETT, L., *Childcare Now: A Survey of Placement Patterns*, British Agencies for Adoption and Fostering (BAAF), London, 1989.

RUSHTON, A., TRESEDER, J. and QUINTON, D., *New Parents for Older Children*, BAAF, London, 1988.

RUSHTON, A., TRESEDER, J. and QUINTON, D., 'Sibling groups in permanent placement', *Adoption and Fostering*, **13**: 4, 5–10, 1989.

RYAN, T. and WALKER, R., *Making Life Story Books*, BAAF, London, 1985 and 1993.

SAINSBURY, E., *Social Work with Families*, Routledge and Kegan Paul, 1975.

SELLICK, C.W., *Supporting Short Term Foster Carers*, Avebury, Aldershot, 1992.

SHAW, M., *Family Placement for Children in Care*, BAAF, London, 1985.

SHAW, M., and HIPGRAVE, T., *Specialist Fostering*, Batsford, 1983.

SHAW, M., and HIPGRAVE, T., 'Specialist Fostering in 1988: A Research Study', *Adoption and Fostering*, **13**: 3, 17–21, 1989a.

SHAW, M., and HIPGRAVE, T., 'Young People and Their Carers in Specialist Fostering', *Adoption and Fostering*, **13**: 4, 11–17, 1989b.

SHELDON, B., *Behaviour Modification*, Tavistock, London, 1986.

SINCLAIR, R., *Decision Making in Statutory Reviews on Children in Care*, Gower, 1985.

SMITH, B., 'Something you do for love: the question of money and foster care', *Adoption and Fostering*, **12**: 4, 34–37, 1988.

SMITH, C., *Adoption and Fostering*, MacMillan, London, 1984.

SMITH, C., 'Restoring Children from Foster Care to their Families', in MARSH, P. and TRISELIOTIS, J., eds., *Prevention and Reunification in Child Care*, Batsford, 1993.

SMITH, G. and CORDEN, J., 'The Introduction of Contracts in a Family Service Unit', *British Journal of Social Work*, **11**: 289–313, 1981.

SOUTHON, V., *Children in Care: Paying Their New Families*, DHSS, HMSO, 1986.

STEIN, T.J. and GAMBRILL, E.D., *A Training Manual*. University of California Press, Berkeley, California, 1976.

STONE, J., *Children in Care: The role of short-term fostering*, Newcastle upon Tyne Social Services Department, 1990.

STONE, N. and STONE, S., 'The prediction of successful foster placement', *Social Casework*, **64**: 1, 11–17, 1983.

STRATHCLYDE SOCIAL WORK DEPARTMENT, *Temporary Fostering*, Unpublished, 1988.

STRATHCLYDE SOCIAL WORK DEPARTMENT, *The Permanent Placements in Adoption and Fostering*, Scottish Office, Central Research Unit, 1991.

TAYLOR-BROWN, S., 'The impact of AIDS on foster care: a family centred approach to services in the United States', *Child Welfare*, **60**: 2, 1991.

THOBURN, J., *Captive Clients*, Routledge and Kegan Paul, London, 1980.

THOBURN, J., *Success and failure in permanent family placement*, Avebury, Aldershot, 1990.

THOBURN, J., 'Permanent Family Placement and the Children Act 1989: Implications for Foster Carers and Social Workers', *Adoption and Fostering*, **15**: 4, 9–12, 1991a.

THOBURN, J., 'The Children Act 1989: Balancing child welfare with the concept of partnership with parents', *Journal of Social Welfare and Family Law*, **5**: 331–344, 1991b.

THOBURN, J., MURDOCK, A., and O'BRIEN, A., *Permanence in Child Care*, Basil Blackwell, Oxford, 1986.

THORNE, B., *Person-Centred Counselling: Therapeutic and Spiritual Dimensions*, Whurr Publications, 1991.

THORPE, R., 'The experiences of children and parents living apart', in TRISELIOTIS, J., ed., *New Development in Foster Care and Adoption*, Routledge and Kegan Paul, 1980.

THORPE, R., 'The Social and Psychological Situation of the long-term Foster Child with regard to his Natural Family', PhD thesis, Nottingham University, 1974.

TOBIS, D., *The Foster Care Pyramid: Factors Associated with the Abuse and Neglect of Children in Foster Boarding Homes*, Human Services Administration, New York, 1982.

TRASLER, G., *In place of parents*, Routledge and Kegan Paul, London, 1960.

TRIETLINE, P., 'Foster Care', in *Collected Papers, First International Conference on Foster Care*, National Foster Care Association (NFCA), London, 1980.

TRISELIOTIS, J., *In Search of Origins*, Routledge and Kegan Paul, 1973.

TRISELIOTIS, J., *Growing Up in Foster Care and After*, Report to the Economic and Social Research Council, London, 1980.

TRISELIOTIS, J., *Group Work in Adoption and Foster Care*, Batsford, 1988.

TRISELIOTIS, J., 'Foster Care Outcomes: A Review of Key Research Findings', *Adoption and Fostering*, **13**: 3, 5–16, 1989.

TUNNARD, J., 'Setting the Scene for Partnership', in Family Rights Group, ed., *The Children Act 1989; Working in Partnership with Families*, HMSO, 1991.

VERITY, P., 'The social fund and foster care allowances', *Adoption and Fostering*, **12**: 2, 3–4, 1988.

VON ARNIM, I., 'Fostering Adolescents – Effects on the Host Children', MSc dissertation, Oxford University, 1988.

WALSH, J.A., 'Risk Factors, Superior Adoptive Capacity and Characteristics of the Foster Home as Predictors of Maintenance of Foster Placement', University of Montana, Paper presented at Western Psychological Association, Los Angeles, April, 1981.

WARD, M., 'Choosing Adoptive Families for Large Sibling Groups', *Child Welfare*, **66**: 3, 249–68, May–June, 1987.

WARHAM, J., *An Introduction to Administration for Social Workers*, Routledge and Kegan Paul, 1975.

WATERHOUSE, S., 'How Foster Carers View Contact', *Adoption and Fostering*, **16**: 2, 42–47, 1992.

WEBB, S. and ALDGATE, J., 'Using Respite Care to Prevent Long-Term Family Breakdown', *Adoption and Fostering*, **15**: 1, 6–13, 1991.

WEDGE, P. and MANTLE, G., *Sibling Groups and Social Work*, Avebury, Aldershot, 1991.

WEINSTEIN, E.A., *The Self-Image of the Foster Child*, Russell Sage Foundation, New York, 1960.

WEST, J., 'Play work and play therapy: distinctions and definitions', *Adoption and Fostering*, **14**: 4, 31–37, 1990.

WESTACOTT, J., *Bridge to Calmer Waters*. Barnardo's, London, 1988.

WHITAKER, D.S., COOK, J.M., DUNN, C. and ROCKLIFFE, S., 'The Experience of Residential Care from the Perspective of Children, Parents and Caregivers', Report to the ESRC, University of York, 1985.

WILKINSON, C., 'Prospect, process and outcome in foster care', M.Phil Thesis, Edinburgh University, 1988.

WINNICOTT, C., 'Face-to-Face with Children', in BRITISH AGENCIES FOR ADOPTION AND FOSTERING, eds, *Working with Children*, BAAF, London, 1984.

WIRES, E.M., 'Some factors in the worker-foster parent relationship', *Child Welfare*, **33**: 8,13, 1985.

WOODMAN, E., 'Access Visits in Family Rights Groups', in FAMILY RIGHTS GROUP, ed., Fostering Parental Contact, Family Rights Group, London, 1982.

YATES, P., 'Post-Placement Support for Adoptive Families of Hard-to-Place Children', MSc dissertation, University of Edinburgh, 1985.

INDEX